The Mythical World of Atlantis

Theories of the Lost Empire from Plato to Disney

A New and Revised Edition of the Classic 1915 Volume
The Mythical World of Atlantis
Theories of the Lost Empire
by Preston B. Whitmore

Revised and updated
by Professor Kyle Van Mitchell,
Ph.D., ASJA, WGAw
Director, Preston B. Whitmore Archives

A Publication of
Whitmore Industries, Ltd.
Information Bureau

a welcome book

EDITIONS

new york

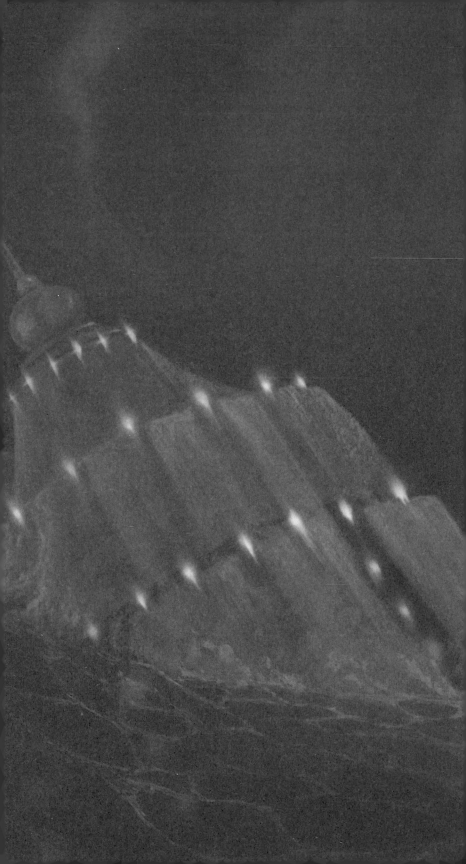

CONTENTS

Introduction to the Revised and Updated Edition
by Professor Kyle Van Mitchell, Ph.D., ASJA, WGAw

For decades, the 1915 publication of *The Mythical World of Atlantis: Theories of the Lost Empire* by Preston B. Whitmore was regarded as a landmark in the study of the history and lore of Atlantis.

What was not known at the time of that volume's appearance was that many of the "theories" espoused by Preston Whitmore were actually facts based on firsthand knowledge gathered by his own expedition—an expedition that Whitmore publicly proclaimed a failure!

The rumors since the publication of the 1915 edition, and the discoveries that have been made public within the last few years about the fateful Whitmore Expedition of 1914 (the events depicted in the recent feature motion picture *Atlantis: The Lost Empire*), led to the decision by the information bureau of Whitmore Industries, Ltd. to revisit the classic 1915 text, with the goal of reestablishing the work's status as the authoritative primer on the lost empire.

Whitmore's heirs thought it fitting that their founder's definitive text on Atlantis should be revised, updated, and expanded to include the startling findings made possible by Preston B. Whitmore himself, and to exhibit those discoveries in a status commensurate with those of other great explorers, historians, archaeologists, scholars—even frauds and dreamers.

It has been my pleasure to work from as strong a foundation as Preston B. Whitmore's own manuscript for the 1915 edition in bringing this fundamental work up to date for a new generation of readers.

Sincerely,

Kyle Van Mitchell, Director
Preston B. Whitmore Archives

Introduction to the 1915 Edition

October 21, 1914

Dear Reader,

It was my great fortune many years ago in my youth to make the acquaintance of one Thaddeus T. Thatch. While I had an interest in the study of commerce, Thatch was always fascinated with the fringes of archaeology. We studied at Georgetown and became the closest of friends. I would bore him with stories of railroad fortunes, factories, and industrial development, and he would respond with theories of lost civilizations: the Anasazi, Lemuria, Mu, and of course his obsession, Atlantis.

The story of Atlantis is history's greatest jigsaw puzzle, but Thatch's passion and his superior intellect held him in good stead, and we are now the beneficiaries of his years of research and sleuthing. Thatch's documents, along with the work of his fine grandson Milo James Thatch, have withstood time and scholastic scrutiny (including an exhaustive factual audit by the New England Academic Consortium) to become recognized as the definitive history of the lost empire.

Within these pages, I have attempted to organize the decisive and determinate Thatch data within a framework of the entire mythological history of the Lost Empire, to create both a basic primer for the uninitiated and a solid reference for the Atlantis scholar.

It is my hope that this reservoir of knowledge will serve as both a document of education and elucidation, and a fitting tribute to the memory of those great explorers and my dear friends Thaddeus T. and Milo J. Thatch.

With warmest regards,

Preston B. Whitmore

Preston Whitmore
Whitmore Industries

An Atlantis Primer

*The who, what, when,
where, why, and
how of Atlantis*

*We've all heard the legend of Atlantis, a continent somewhere in the
mid-Atlantic that was home to an advanced civilization, possessing
technology far beyond our own, that, according to Plato, was suddenly struck by some cataclysmic event that sank it beneath the sea.
It's just a myth isn't it? Pure fantasy? Well, that is where you would
be wrong.*

*Ten thousand years before the Egyptians built the pyramids, the
Atlanteans had electricity, advanced medicine—even the power of
flight! Impossible, you say? Not for them. Numerous ancient cultures
all over the globe agree that Atlantis possessed a power source of some
kind, more powerful than steam, coal, even our modern internal
combustion engines. I propose that we find Atlantis, find that power
source and bring it back to the surface!*

—Discovered in the notes of Milo James Thatch, 1914

ATLANTIS. It's the kind of word that evokes as many different responses as there are different kinds of people. To the
romantic, it may conjure up dreamy images of a lost paradise
of peace. To the skeptic, it probably conjures up a thousand
questions with no concrete answers. To the man in the street,
it might be a half-remembered story heard in his far-off youth
—or an absolutely real place that Uncle Sid visited last summer. Well, you know how people are.

Did the lost continent of Atlantis really exist, or is the well-
known story of an island utopia destroyed by cataclysm only a
fable?[1]

---

[1] Coined in the writings of Sir Thomas More, the word *utopia* literally
translates from the Greek as "no place."

The story of Atlantis was first told by the Greek philosopher Plato (c. 427 B.C. – 347 B.C.) in 360 B.C., in his dialogues the *Timaeus* and the *Critias*. Although Plato used Atlantis as an allegory, to teach the perils of greed, insolence, and brutality, and to demonstrate the punishment meted out by heaven to those who worship false gods, he also asserted that the foundational story was *true*.

His tale "has the great advantage of being a fact and not a fiction," Plato says, a shared memory of a catastrophe of such epic scale that it had been passed down by word of mouth for centuries. Myth or reality, the legend of Atlantis has echoed through almost every known culture on earth, and inspired a search that has persisted ever since.

For the sake of brevity and clarity, the following information about Atlantis has been assembled in digest form. In this manner, many of the rudiments of Atlantean history can be established, so that the more detailed information to come will have some foundation for the uninitiated reader. Experts and scholars can skip or skim this part, but I wouldn't recommend it.[2]

What Was Atlantis?

Atlantis was a continent of the Atlantic Ocean. Again according to Plato, an advanced civilization developed and flourished on the island continent some 11, 600 years ago. Most modern science rejects the historical existence of Atlantis, as it has so far been unable to find any traces of it—much as the existence of Homer's mythic Troy was rejected by science until its ruins were discovered by archaeologist Heinrich Schliemann in 1872.[3]

---

[2] Preston Whitmore was rather renowned for speaking his mind.

[3] Here Whitmore reveals a cagey attitude regarding his telling of the mythology of Atlantis. At the time of this writing, he knew better than any man alive the truth regarding the lost empire, but here proves that his legendary reputation as both a poker player and a prankster was well earned.

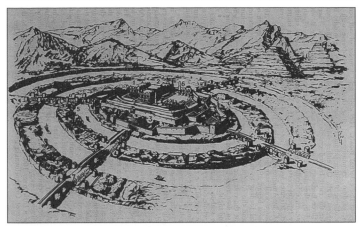

The Atlantean capital as described by Plato. Rendering by R. Avotin.

What Was Atlantis Like?

Plato described Atlantis as a land of plenty, a true earthly paradise where want was unknown and peace was a way of life. The island itself was a great lush plain surrounded on three sides by immense embracing mountains. The excellent soil nourished all manner of trees and plants, and the continent bloomed with bountiful flora, all of which contributed to a rich agriculture.

Wealthy villages and hamlets could be found in the hills and mountains, and their meadows, woods, and fields were home to an amazing variety of animals.[4]

Atlantis had a great capital (also called Atlantis), a walled city comprising grand buildings made of red, black, and white stone. The capital was laid out in five concentric circles, with a great citadel or palace at its center point. The entire outer wall was described as having a coating of brass, with a second, interior wall coated with tin, and a third wall, the one enclosing the palace, that glittered with the red light of a now unknown element called oricalcum.[5]

---

[4] For example, Plato mentions elephants, one of only two known references to these animals in extant Greek literature.

[5] This precious mineral, which the inhabitants regarded as highly as gold, was mined in underground caverns.

The citizens of Atlantis led a very active civic life. Among the buildings of Atlantis, there were many temples dedicated to many gods, and there were verdant public and private gardens all about. Gathering places such as markets, baths, gymnasiums, footracing courses, and even a horseracing track were all part of the public space in Atlantis.

A bustling seaport filled with merchant vessels and seamen fronted the city. Atlantean trade routes were purported to span the globe, preceding an Atlantean empire that would rise around the world.

Map of the Atlantean continent showing the extent of Ice Age glaciation.

A central canal three hundred feet wide and a hundred feet deep entered the city from the sea, large enough for any vessel to find its way to a sheltered interior harbor. The rest of the city was also accessible by water: a complex series of canals provided key transportation routes throughout the metropolis as well as irrigation for the fertile plain from plentiful mountain waters.

Finally, the Atlanteans possessed one of the greatest treasures of all time, and their civilization held material wealth and precious objects beyond those of any culture before or since.

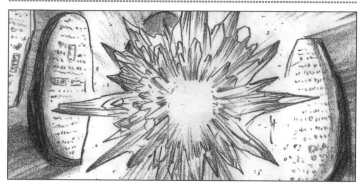

Did the Atlanteans Know of a Mighty Power Source?

It is said that tens of thousands of years ago, a giant comet passed close to the earth, and a piece of this comet fell on the land mass inhabited by the Atlanteans. This ordinary race of people became extremely powerful when they discovered that the comet fragment possessed great properties. It soon became their power source.

To a large degree, the comet fragment even became a deity. The main crystal hewn from it became like a power plant, a giant amorphous ball of light that floated high above the city, giving its light and life to all. In turn, each Atlantean wore a small shard of the mother crystal around his or her neck. This personal crystal was used for healing and was found to bring unusually long life. It was constantly recharged by the mother crystal, or, as the Atlanteans called it, "the Heart of Atlantis." [6]

Who Were the Atlantean People?

For long ages, no one can say for sure, the Atlantean people appreciated their blessings of abundance and lived self-sufficiently, and at peace with the rest of the world. They were untainted by their possessions and great wealth, and spent their lives engaged in activities of generosity and gentility. Their primary avocations were education, cultivating virtue, and living

---

[6] Again, foxy Whitmore asserts as an accepted component of Atlantean lore knowledge that only *he* was truly privy to at the time of his writing!

in peace with each other and in harmony with nature.

What Happened to Atlantis and its People?

Plato reports that Atlantis disappeared into the sea in 9000 B.C. as the result of a worldwide volcanic cataclysm.[7]

Over time, it is said, the Atlanteans had begun to use their technological power to dominate other civilizations. They used the crystal to fuel a powerful armada and waged war with astounding ferocity, but their hubris caused a great accident, and the power of the crystals wiped the Atlanteans off the face of the earth. The benevolent crystals are said to have saved Atlantis with a massive force field, but the holocaust drove Atlantis deep into the center of the earth and caused a great flood to sweep over all the earth. (The flood was memorialized in the biblical book of Genesis.)

By some accounts, the ancient leaders of Atlantis vowed to keep the power of the crystals a secret forever to prevent a recurrence of this traumatic time. All accounts of history were destroyed, and the crystal was hidden deep beneath the city of Atlantis, where it was meant to stay forever, like a genie in a bottle.

Whatever the specific cataclysm, Plato placed the destruction of Atlantis in about 9000 B.C. Now this of course places Atlantis, with its enormously sophisticated culture and technology, at a zenith of sophistication and prosperity millennia before ancient Troy!

There are also those who maintain that Plato exaggerated quite a bit, sometimes to see if his students were paying atten-

---

[7] Psychic healer and prophet Edgar Cayce (1877–1945) believed that the destruction of the Atlantean civilization was as much a cultural collapse as a physical one. He also declared that prior to its destruction earthquakes divided the Atlantean continent into five islands, the largest of which was known as Poseida. Cayce said that as the Atlanteans departed their vanishing continent, they spread far and wide in missionary fashion, teaching the natives they encountered, so that their great civilization would not be lost. Cayce believed this theory explains ancestral similarities in such diverse cultures as Native America, Egypt, Morocco, and Central America.

tion, sometimes to shroud the factual origins of his teachings in order to play up their mythic qualities.[8]

What Historical Records of Atlantis Exist?

Plato is the primary source of any knowledge of Atlantis anywhere close to the era of its existence—even if he wrote of it *centuries* after its zenith.

Plato had overheard the legend as a boy, during a dinner where his teacher and mentor Socrates (469–399 B.C.) held forth with a detailed account of the lost civilization. The legend was generations old when Socrates told it, handed down by a Greek sage and lawgiver named Solon (? – c. 550 B.C.), a contemporary of Plato's great-great-grandfather. Solon was a poet, a statesman, and one of the seven sages of ancient Greece, who had brought the story back from a pilgrimage to Egypt, where he was shown antique documents in the holy shrine of the ancient Egyptian capital—annals of an empire that had dominated the entire world 9,000 years earlier.

The descriptions of Atlantis given to Solon by the Egyptian priests are the starting points of the legends of Atlantis that persist to this day. Strangely enough, Plato stopped his history of Atlantis without finishing it—the account actually ends in mid-*sentence*. He never returned to the fascinating story.

What's more, after the *Timaeus* and the *Critias*, there are no further renditions of Atlantean myth. There are not multiple retellings of the Atlantis story as there are multiple versions of the Trojan War or Jason and the Golden Fleece, or other well-known tales of Greek mythology. After the collapse of the Roman Empire, much of the knowledge and culture of antiquity were lost. The telling of the tales of Atlantis begins with Solon, Socrates, and Plato—and then vanishes into the shadows of the Dark Ages.

---

[8] As author Robert Sullivan succinctly explains in *Atlantis Rising* (1999), "He was stretching a truth to get at a greater truth."

Plato and Socrates with a Side of Solon

Until Thaddeus Thatch started rattling my head with endless discussion of all things ancient, Plato, Socrates, and Solon were just some old fellows with beards wearing togas. I learned a little more about them, and they became rather more interesting. Here are a few pointers about the old gents. I suggest that a little further study about such fellows wouldn't do you a bit of harm, either.

Plato was a philosopher, born on or around May 21, 427 B.C. in Athens. (Don't ask me how anyone knows the date). The son of Athenian aristocrats, he lived his whole life in Athens. Little is known of his early years, but he was given the finest education Athens had to offer, and he devoted himself to politics and writing. His acquaintance with Socrates changed his life; the two became close associates. Plato proved to be the most outstanding among Socrates' pupils and adherents.

Before he died in 347 B.C., Plato founded a significant philosophical school, which would exist for almost a thousand years thereafter. His system attracted many followers in the centuries after his death, and reappeared as the great rival of early Christianity, *Neoplatonism*.

Socrates was another Athenian philosopher. With his doctrines and character immortalized in Plato's dialogues, his influence on Western philosophy is immeasurable. Plato wrote extensively of his mentor's philosophical technique, the Socratic method, which was to ask for definitions of morally significant concepts such as Justice, and, by extracting incongruities from the responses, to expose the ignorance of the respondent and elicit a deeper exploration of the concepts themselves. Socrates was tried on charges of "impiety and corruption of youth" by defenders of a restored democracy in Athens. Found guilty, he was put to death by being forced to drink hemlock.

Solon was an Athenian statesman and poet. His many legal, constitutional, and economic reforms paved the way for the development of democracy in Athens. Enslavement for debt was abolished, and citizenship granted to foreign craftsmen settling in Athens. Wealth rather than birth was made the criterion for participation in political life, and inhumane legal codes were generally abandoned.

Literary Atlantis

From Plato's Timaeus *and* Critias *(360 B.C.)*
to Jules Verne's 20,000 Leagues Under
the Sea *(1870), and beyond*

Plato's Timaeus *and* Critias

FROM THE EGYPTIAN PRIEST, who told Solon; to Solon, who told Socrates; to Socrates, who was overheard by the young Plato, the legend of Atlantis reveals a rich oral tradition. It appears that Plato was simply the first fellow to write it down, in a pair of dialogues titled the *Timaeus* and the *Critias*, thus establishing the foundation for everything that was written down afterward.

The dialogues consist of conversations between Socrates, Timaeus, Critias, and Hermocrates, following Socrates' description of his idea of the perfect state.

Timaeus relates a story that begins on a grand scale—the cosmic origins of the universe. Eventually his narrative focuses down to a tale of men, the story of the strife between the ancient Athenians and the Atlanteans, purported to have occurred 9,000 years before Plato's time.

Many believe the tale to be nothing more than a simple fiction, an imaginary creation used to illustrate a philosophical point. Others believe that the story was an embellished retelling of actual events that may have destroyed the Minoan civilization on Crete and Thera (one theory being that the facts were purposely obscured and exaggerated by Plato). Still others maintain that the story is an accurate historical and factual representation of a long lost and almost completely forgotten land.[9]

Here is the gist of the information contained in Plato's dialogues:

More than ten centuries ago, there flourished an island nation located in the Atlantic Ocean and populated by a noble and powerful race.

Atlantis was the dominion of Poseidon, god of the sea. Poseidon fell in love with a mortal woman named Cleito, and in order to protect her the god established a citadel, surrounded by concentric rings of water and land, on a hilltop.

Cleito gave birth to five pairs of twin boys, who became the first rulers of Atlantis. The island was divided among the brothers with the eldest, Atlas, first king of Atlantis, being

given domain over the central hill and its environs.

In homage to Poseidon, a temple was built at the top of the central hill. Here the rulers of Atlantis assembled to discuss laws, pass judgments, and pay tribute to Poseidon in the shadow of a giant golden statue of the god astride a chariot borne by winged horses.

The island was a hub for trade and commerce, and its rulers not only governed the people and dominion of their own continent but maintained far-flung outposts through Europe and Africa.

The great natural resources found on their island home satisfied all the wants the population could have, but the civ-

---

9   As famous as it is as the source of all written records of Atlantis, the majority of Plato's *Timaeus* is concerned with a theological chronicle of the origin of the world and wonders of nature, not with the "story of Atlantis," as is often believed.

ilization was also endowed with enormous wealth and treasure of precious metals and stones.

Water was central to the lives of the Atlantean populace. The sea surrounded them, and a canal, hewn through the rings of land and water, flowed south for five miles to the sea to facilitate transit and trade.

Layed out just outside the moated citadel was the capital city of Atlantis, a densely populated area where most of the population lived. The capital, also named Atlantis, extended across the plain for eleven miles.

Beyond the capital lay a gigantic fertile plain three hundred miles long and one hundred miles wide, behind which majestic mountains soared to the skies. Lakes, rivers, woodlands, and meadows dotted the mountains, as did several villages and hamlets. An irrigation canal, used to accumulate water from the rivers and streams of the surrounding mountain, encircled the plain.

The benevolent climate made two annual harvests possible. The natural rains nourished the winter harvest, while the summer harvest was sustained by irrigation from the canals. In addition to the grain harvests, the island provided a variety of herbs, fruits, and nuts. A number of species of trees provided various kinds of wood. An abundance of wild animals, including game animals and even elephants, roamed the island.

The Atlantean people lived uncomplicated and virtuous lives, but over the course of generations, greed and power slowly began to corrupt them. Finally, beleaguered by the escalating immorality of the Atlanteans, Zeus and the other gods convened to determine a fitting punishment.

Soon, in one violent cataclysm, Atlantis was gone, chastened by the angry gods and engulfed by the furious ocean.

That's pretty much the story told by Plato around 360 B.C. in his dialogues, and subsequent stories of Atlantis rarely stray very far in overall content from what Plato wrote.

There may be changes in time frames, global location, or other details, but Plato's vision of Atlantis remains with us centuries after it was written.

The Timaeus and the *Critias* were actually intended to be the first two parts of a trilogy, but Plato never finished the ambitious work.[10] The *Timaeus* and the half-finished *Critias* are all that exist of the promising trilogy.

After the *Timaeus* and the *Critias*, there are no further literary renditions of Atlantean myth (although many of its elements survived the Dark Ages through oral tradition). Aristotle dismissed Plato's tale as a pure fantasy, and the literary life of the great legend went fallow for two thousand years or so.

Atlantis: The Antediluvian World by Ignatius Donnelly (1882)

A couple of millennia passed. Then, along came a man named Ignatius Donnelly. Born in Philadelphia, Donnelly was an original, one of those great American entrepreneurs who failed at nearly every rational and constructive thing he tried, and became rich and famous from a crazy avocation. (Not that there's a thing *wrong* about such activity.)[11]

Donnelly was a lawyer with utopian aspirations, and he moved to Minnesota in 1856 to promote a utopian commune (some called it a simple land-development scheme) known as Nininger City. When Nininger City was left with but one citizen, namely Ignatius Donnelly, he switched careers, this time to farming, and also began to dabble in politics. He was elected lieutenant governor of Minnesota in 1859, and again in 1861.

Donnelly entered political life for two primary reasons.

---

[10] After Critias' tale of Atlantis, Hermocrates was to finish the cycle.

[11] Here Whitmore certainly speaks from a variety of his own experiences.

He is said to have been a mesmerizing orator, and he had some political views that were fairly radical, especially to a nation embroiled in a bloody civil war. He joined the Republican Party because of its stand against slavery and was elected to the U.S. House of Representatives (Minnesota, 1863–1869).

He supported the Radical Republicans in their policy of chastening the defeated Confederate states, and was instrumental in establishing the National Bureau of Education to help people of all races obtain an education. In the years that followed, he formed the Independent Anti-Monopoly Party (1877), the Populist Party (1891), and ran (unsuccessfully) for Congress.

He was ahead of his time on many issues, but he had one important flaw. He simply seemed to lack the ability to get things done.

In the early 1880s, during a respite between failed ventures, he began to ponder one of his longtime interests. As a child, Donnelly had read the dialogues of Plato, and the descriptions of Atlantis and its demise had fascinated him ever since.

In the mid-1870s, the world had been rocked by an archaeological revelation that rewrote history books: German businessman and archaeologist Heinrich Schliemann's discovery of the ruins of Troy. Like Plato's Atlantis, Homer's Troy had, until that time, been considered nothing but a fiction.

Galvanized by Schliemann's find,[12] Donnelly was struck by an idea. If a careful rereading of Homer could lead to the discovery of the real Troy, then, by thunder, a careful rereading of Plato could lead to the discovery of the real Atlantis!

During years of research, Donnelly was impressed by the historical similarity of plants, animals, and cultures on either

---

[12] Which was motivated for the most part by Charles McLaren's 1822 book *A Dissertation on the Topography of the Plains of Troy.*

side of the Atlantic Ocean. "We find on both sides of the Atlantic precisely the same arts, sciences, religious beliefs, habits, customs, and traditions," Donnelly writes. "It is absurd to say that the people of the two continents arrived *separately* at precisely the same ends." He noted the similarity between the pyramids of Egypt and those in Mexico, and cited the similarities in their writing systems or hieroglyphics.

Donnelly's obsession resulted in the 1882 publication of *Atlantis: the Antediluvian World*, a book that became one of the greatest bestsellers of its age, and sent a shock wave throughout the world. It launched an "Atlantis craze," a cultural interest in and acceptance of all things perceived "Atlantean," that has yet to cease.

In large part, Donnelly's book was a dissection and elaboration of Plato's descriptions of Atlantean geography, architecture, and culture, overlaid with his own findings, and a large measure of conjecture, presented in a prose style of great scholarly authority, so that many of the book's hundreds of thousands of readers took Donnelly's speculations as academic fact. It also began a tradition of "armchair exploration" and homegrown intellectual research that persists to this day.[13]

Donnelly's work was discussed and debated in salons, offices, and classrooms around the world, and a man who had failed at everything he had tried to do suddenly found himself both a celebrity (Donnelly even received a correspondence from the British Prime Minister supporting the "findings" in his book!), and quite wealthy.

Donnelly grew accustomed to his role as a sort of erudite literary explorer. In 1887 he published *Ragnarok: The Age of Fire and Gravel*,[14] in which he asserted that clay, gravel, and decomposed rocks characteristic of the drift age were the result of contact between the earth and a comet. In *The Great*

---

[13] Donnelly's work predated by a century a similar publishing craze of the 1970s, which has been labeled "pseudo-science." Its most famous product is arguably *Chariots of the Gods?* by Erich von Daniken.

Cryptogram (1888) he posited that Francis Bacon wrote the plays of Shakespeare. In 1891, he wrote a gloomy futuristic novel, *Caesar's Column*, predicting a twentieth-century USA dominated by the rich and corrupt.[15]

Donnelly returned to politics—where he failed again—and died in 1901. But he had placed a notion in the collective mind that had a life far beyond his own, an idea that remains alive to this day. Ignatius Donnelly was the father of serious discourse on Atlantis, now widely known as Atlantology.

Isis Unveiled *by Helena Petrovna Blavatsky (1877)*

Helena Petrovna Blavatsky, better known as Madame Blavatsky (1831–1891) was as much a character as Donnelly, if not more. (There will be much more about this eccentric personality in the "Spiritual Atlantis" section). Blavatsky founded a philosophical organization called the Theosophical Society, which included in its order of Cosmic Masters Jesus Christ, Buddha, Confucius, Solomon and…Plato.

Atlantis was first brought to the attention of the West by Plato, and Madame Blavatsky maintained that Plato was a theosophical initiate and obtained the information about Atlantis presented in the *Timaeus* and the *Critias* as part of his theosophical initiation. Blavatsky explained that his attribution of his source to Socrates and Solon was intended to disguise the true origin of his wisdom.

Blavatsky mentions Atlantis numerous times in her first major literary work, *Isis Unveiled*, first published in 1877. In its 1,200 pages, she explores the mysteries of ancient and modern science and theology. Throughout her exploration of the universal truths of the ancient wisdom tradition,

---

[14] In Norse mythology, Ragnarok is doomsday, on which the gods of Asgard, led by Odin, would fight the forces of evil, led by Loki. After the battle, the universe would be destroyed by fire and a new golden age would commence.

[15] Some would call this clairvoyant.

Blavatsky scatters hints and details of Atlantis, and affirms the island's existence:

> *The perfect identity of the rites, ceremonies, traditions, and even the names of the deities, among the Mexicans and ancient Babylonians and Egyptians, is a sufficient proof of South America being peopled by a colony which mysteriously found its way across the Atlantic. When? At what period? History is silent on that point; but those who consider that there is no tradition, sanctified by ages, without a certain sediment of truth at the bottom of it, believe in the Atlantis legend. There are, scattered throughout the world, a handful of thoughtful and solitary students, who pass their lives in obscurity. These men believe the story of the Atlantis to be no fable, but maintain that at different epochs of the past huge islands, and even continents, existed where now there is but a wild waste of waters.*

Sir Francis Bacon

Theosophists and other followers of Madame Blavatsky wonder to this day: Did Ignatius Donnelly read *Isis Unveiled* and then commence the research for his own book, which although far more widely read was, after all, published five years after Blavatsky's? Why did his book appear so soon after hers, when public interest in the subject of Atlantis had all but lapsed for twenty-two centuries?

Here's an interesting piece of the puzzle: *Isis Unveiled* quotes page 179 of John D. Baldwin's *Prehistoric Nations* on the origin of the name *Atlantis*.[16] Baldwin traces the name

---

[16] A mid-19th century archaeologist, author, and historian, John D. Baldwin wrote *Pre-Historic Nations* (1869) which is oft mentioned in historical documents of the 1870s on the discovery of Troy. Baldwin is also the author of *Ancient America, in Notes on American Archaeology* (1871).

not to the Greek *Atlas*, but to the Central American word *atl*, meaning "water" and "war."

Five years later, in his *Atlantis: The Antediluvian World*, Donnelly references the same quote from Baldwin in his chapter "Corroborating Circumstances."

And six years after Donnelly's book, Blavatsky published *The Secret Doctrine: The Synthesis of Science, Religion, and Philosophy*, praising Donnelly's book and directing still more attention to it.

Theosophists argue, "Would it not be fair to say that while Donnelly wrote the seminal book on the specific subject of Atlantis, Blavatsky, with all the worldwide attention she received, should be the one to receive the true credit for initially igniting the present-day interest in the subject?"

I think not.

Jules Verne, 20,000 Leagues Under the Sea, *and the Atlantis Mania*

For the observant reader who might have been wondering what I'm up to, there is a reason for the reverse chronology you might have noticed. Donnelly was without question the most famous and influential chronicler of Atlantis in the nineteenth century, and it seems apparent that Blavatsky was at least a research source for Donnelly if not a direct inspiration—but both were beaten to the worldwide punch on Atlantis by a true (and still celebrated) maestro of his domain, Jules Verne.

Verne was a writer, born in Nantes, France. He studied law in Paris, then turned his attention to writing. From 1848 he wrote opera libretti, then in 1863 developed a new vein in fiction in the novel *Cinq semaines en ballon (Five Weeks in a Balloon)*. Anticipating the possibilities of science, exaggerating or dramatizing certain of their components, and surrounding the scientific machinery with colorful characters and a gentle breath of fantasy, Verne all but invented what we know today as science fiction. Verne also greatly influenced the early science fiction of H.G. Wells.

Among his immortal books are *Voyage au centre de la terre* (1864; *Journey to the Centre of the Earth*), *De la terre à la lune* (1865; *From the Earth to the Moon*), *Le tour du monde en quatre-vingt jours* (1873; *Around the World in Eighty Days*), *L'Île mystérieuse* (1874; *The Mysterious Island*).

Oh, yes. And *Vingt mille lieues sous les mers* (1870; *Twenty Thousand Leagues Under the Sea*). It is perhaps the most popular book of Verne's entire science-fiction oeuvre, *Voyages extraordinaires* (1863–1910). In the story, Professor Pierre Aronnax, the narrator of the story, boards an American frigate commissioned to investigate a series of attacks on international shipping by what is thought to be a giant sea monster. The supposed creature is revealed to be a submarine boat called *Nautilus*, which sinks Aronnax's vessel. The survivors meet the submarine's captain, a mysterious misanthrope who imprisons Arronax, his devoted servant Conseil, along with Ned Land, a temperamental harpooner. Over the following year, Captain Nemo[17] leads the three captives on a

---

[17] *Nemo* is from Latin, meaning "no one."

worldwide underwater adventure.

Arronax describes the beginning of an unusual excursion:

> *That night, about eleven o'clock, I received a most unex-*
> *pected visit from Captain Nemo. He asked me very gra-*
> *ciously if I felt fatigued from my watch of the preceding*
> *night. I answered in the negative.*
>
> *"Then, M. Aronnax, I propose a curious excursion."*
>
> *"Propose, Captain?"*
>
> *"You have hitherto only visited the submarine depths by*
> *daylight, under the brightness of the sun. Would it suit you*
> *to see them in the darkness of the night?"*
>
> *"Most willingly."*
>
> *"I warn you, the way will be tiring. We shall have far to*
> *walk, and must climb a mountain. The roads are not well*
> *kept."*
>
> *"What you say, Captain, only heightens my curiosity; I*
> *am ready to follow you."*
>
> *"Come then, sir, we will put on our diving-dresses."*

The Captain and Arronax set off on their excursion, which, as Nemo has promised, is lengthy and circuitous, but filled with curious and startling sights. Finally, the two explorers reach their destination:

> *There indeed under my eyes, ruined, destroyed, lay a*
> *town—its roofs open to the sky, its temples fallen, its arches*
> *dislocated, its columns lying on the ground, from which*
> *one would still recognize the massive character of Tuscan*
> *architecture. Further on, some remains of a gigantic aque-*
> *duct; here the high base of an Acropolis, with the floating*
> *outline of a Parthenon; there traces of a quay, as if an*
> *ancient port had formerly abutted on the borders of the*
> *ocean, and disappeared with its merchant vessels and its*
> *war-galleys. Farther on again, long lines of sunken walls*
> *and broad, deserted streets—a perfect Pompeii escaped*

beneath the waters. Such was the sight that Captain Nemo brought before my eyes!

Where was I? Where was I? I must know at any cost. I tried to speak, but Captain Nemo stopped me with a gesture, and, picking up a piece of chalkstone, advanced to a rock of black basalt, and traced a single word: ATLANTIS

What a light shot through my mind! Atlantis! The Atlantis of Plato, that continent denied by Origen and Humbolt, who placed its disappearance amongst the legendary tales. I had it there now before my eyes, bearing upon it the unexceptionable testimony of its catastrophe. The region thus engulfed was beyond Europe, Asia, and Libya, beyond the columns of Hercules, where those powerful people, the Atlantides, lived, against whom the first wars of ancient Greeks were waged.

Thus, led by the strangest destiny, I was treading under foot the mountains of this continent, touching with my hand those ruins a thousand generations old and contemporary with the geological epochs. I was walking on the very spot where the contemporaries of the first man had walked.

It is difficult to remember in today's hurly-burly world what a sensation books used to cause fifty years past. But even I remember the sensation that surrounded the publication of *Twenty Thousand Leagues Under the Sea*, and the endless conjecture about its plausibility, the fascinating debate of its exotic technologies, and engaging reverie about its exotic submarine ports of call that this amazing novel caused.

And it came five years before Blavatsky, and ten years before Donnelly. All these books are still in print today, but only one is truly regarded as a timeless popular classic.

This book is one of the common points I shared with Thaddeus Thatch.

A detail of an illustration entitled "A walk at the bottom of the Sea" from Jules Verne's Twenty Thousand Leagues Under the Sea.

Some Other Significant Atlantis Literature

Since the time of Preston Whitmore, there have been hundreds, if not thousands of volumes that use the history or idea of Atlantis as a point of origin. From investigative nonfiction to novels to children's books to business management manuals, literary Atlantis has continued the propagation of the Platonic concepts of the lost empire begun by Verne, Blavatsky, and Donnelly more than a century ago. The complete bibliography of literary Atlantis would fill several volumes of this size, so a simple few reflecting the variety of available Atlantis writings are listed below.

The End of Atlantis by J. V. Luce (1978)
A study of the cause and effect of the eruption of Thera (modern Santorini) in the early fifteenth century B.C. and its connections to descriptions of Plato's Atlantis.

Doomsday, 1999 A.D. by Charles Berlitz (1981)
The man who popularized the Bermuda Triangle and the discovery of Noah's ark investigates theories and prophecies that herald the world's imminent destruction, and arrives at an alarming new prediction. Maps of Atlantis and drawings by J. Manson Valentine.

Atlantis: Myth or Reality? by Murray Hope (1991)
Hope writes authoritatively on the nature of Atlantis and Atlanteans, and of the myths, tales, and traditions that survived around the world after the Golden Age.

Atlantis in America: Navigators of the Ancient World by Ivar Zapp and George Erikson (1997)
New theories regarding the origins of Mesoamerican civilization and its relation to Atlantean tradition. Ideas on ancient navigation provide an understanding of transoceanic contact prior to the age of Columbus.

When the Sky Fell: In Search of Atlantis by Rand Flem-Ath, Rose Flem-Ath (1997)
A fascinating theory about the environmental catastrophe that destroyed Atlantis and how the forces that shattered that great civilization can happen again—and bring the end of the world.

Imagining Atlantis by Richard Ellis (1998)

"Whether its source was extraterrestrial, prehistorical, or imaginary, Atlantis, unique among the Western world's myths, has become a part of our mythohistory," says Ellis. In this book, Ellis traces the conclusions of the most persistent theories of the 2,000 or so scholarly works "proving" that what Plato meant was, variously, the island of Thera (Santorini), Palestine, the Peloponnesian town of Helice, the Americas—or something more bizarre.

Atlantis Rising by Robert Sullivan (1999)

In this volume, Robert Sullivan, who first rose to international prominence with his breakthrough research on Santa Claus, is able to separate historical truth from mere legend, fact from fiction, science from silliness. Delving into the historical record, then into secret files that have long been locked away at the famous Woods Hole Oceanographic Institute, he discovers rare transcripts, documents, maps and, incredibly, photographs. Paintings by the renowned natural-history artist Glenn Wolff.

Atlantis: A Tale of the Earth by Roger J. Didio (1999)

Before Camelot, before Avalon and Middle Earth, there was Atlantis. And now, at the dawn of the Third Millennium, the greatest civilization the world has ever known rises again in an epic fantasy adventure.

Gateway to Atlantis: The Search for the Source of a Lost Civilization by Andrew Collins (2000)

Andrew Collins has gathered convincing evidence that may establish not only that Atlantis did indeed exist but also that remnants of it survive today. "Probably the most substantial and well researched book on Atlantis since Ignatius Donnelly." — Colin Wilson, *London Daily Mail*

The Journal of Milo Thatch assembled, preserved, and annotated by Preston B. Whitmore (2001)

A long-lost personal journal with period annotations by the financier who funded the famed 1914 Whitmore expedition, which set out to find the lost empire. Copiously illustrated with eyewitness drawings, diagrams, and photos.

Unearthing Atlantis by Charles R. Pellegrino (2001)

Updated edition of Pellegrino's 1994 findings in Thera (Santorini). In a synthesis of historical and literary evidence, archaeological and paleontological detective work, the author argues that the Minoan civilization on the Greek islands of Crete and Thera gave rise to the Atlantis myth.

Atlantis on the Screen

In Whitmore's day, the moving picture was a relatively new medium, just beginning to realize its potential. During the years surrounding the Atlantis expedition and the preparation of this volume, Whitmore would probably not have realized that Atlantis had already made its movie debut, in an obscure

1913 Danish silent production. It was the first of many film (and later, television) presentations to use the lost empire as the foundation of a story. The following is a list, in reverse chronological order, of many of the Atlantis-themed movies and TV programs.

Motion Pictures

1. *Atlantis: The Lost Empire* (2001), produced by Don Hahn, directed by Kirk Wise and Gary Trousdale

2. *Quest for Atlantis* (1999), starring James Earl Jones and Jennifer Rubin

3. *Race for Atlantis* (IMAX®, 1998), narrated by Michael Jeter

4. *Humanoids from Atlantis* (1992), from the director who brought you *Zombie Cop*

5. *Atlantis* (1991), a documentary about dolphins directed by Luc Besson;
   a.k.a. *Atlantis – Le Creature del Mare*

6. *Octagon y Atlantis, la revancha* (Mexico, 1991)

7. *Alien from L.A.* (1987), starring Kathy Ireland;
   a.k.a. *Atlantis, den försvunna staden* (Sweden)

8. *I Predatori di Atlantide* (Italy, 1983), starring Christopher Connelly—not really about Atlantis, more about cannibalism;
   a.k.a. *Atlantis,*
   a.k.a. *Atlantis Inferno,*
   a.k.a. *The Atlantis Interceptors,*
   a.k.a. *The Raiders of Atlantis*

9. *The Amazing Captain Nemo* (1978), starring Jose Ferrer, Mel Ferrer, Lynda Day George, and Burgess Meredith;
   a.k.a. *Abenteuer Atlantis* (West Germany, 1978)

10. *The Lost City of Atlantis* (documentary, 1978)

11. *Warlords of Atlantis* (1978), starring Doug McClure, John Ratzenberger, and Cyd Charisse;
    a.k.a. *Seven Cities of Atlantis*

12. *Unterwegs nach Atlantis* (Germany, 1976)

13. *Beyond Atlantis* (1973), starring Patrick Wayne;
    a.k.a. *Sea Creatures*

14. *Männer sind zum Lieben da* (Germany, 1969),
    a.k.a. *Atlantis: Ein Sommermärchen,*
    a.k.a. *The Girls From Atlantis*

15. *Agente 003, Operacion Atlantida* (Italy, Spain, 1965), starring John Ericson of *Bedknobs and Broomsticks* fame

16. *Il Conquistatore di Atlantide* (Italy, 1965),
    a.k.a. *Conqueror of Atlantis,*
    a.k.a. *Kingdom in the Sand*

17. *Atlantis, the Lost Continent* (1961), directed by George Pal, starring Sal Ponti, Edward Platt, Frank DeKova, and Jay Novello

18. *Ercole alla conquista di Atlantide* (Italy, 1961);
    a.k.a. *Hercule à la conquête de l'Atlantide*,
    a.k.a. *Hercules Conquers Atlantis*,
    a.k.a. *Hercules and the Captive Women*,
    a.k.a. *Hercules and the Conquest of Atlantis*,
    a.k.a. *Hercules and the Haunted Women*,
    a.k.a. *Herkules erobert Atlantis*

19. *L'Atlantide* (Italy, 1961), based on the novel by Pierre Benoit, which was also filmed previously in Belgium, 1920; Germany, 1932; USA, 1948;
    a.k.a. *Antinea*,
    a.k.a. *Antinea, l'amante della città sepolta*,
    a.k.a. *Atlantis, City Beneath the Desert*,
    a.k.a. *Journey Beneath the Desert*,
    a.k.a. *Lost Kingdom*,
    a.k.a. *Queen of Atlantis*

20. *Bells of Atlantis* (Denmark, 1952), starring Anaïs Nin as the "Naked Woman in the Hammock"

21. *Siren of Atlantis* (USA, 1948)

22. *Die Herrin von Atlantis* (1932), starring Brigitte Helm, the robot/woman from *Metropolis*;
    a.k.a. *Queen of Atlantis*,
    refilmed as *The Mistress of Atlantis* (1932),
    a.k.a. *The Lost Atlantis* (USA, 1939)

23. *Atlantis* (France, 1930), actually a tale of the *Titanic*

24. *L'Atlantide* (Belgium, 1920);
    a.k.a. *Lost Atlantis* (USA)

25. *Atlantis* (Denmark, 1913), featuring Michael Curtiz, future director of *Casablanca*

Movies for Television

1. *Rock the Boat* (2000), starring Amanda Donohoe of *L.A. Law* fame, and independent film queen Adrienne Shelly; a.k.a. *Atlantis Conspiracy*

2. *Escape From Atlantis* (1997), starring Black Belt Hall of Famer Jeff Speakman, and Tim Thomerson from *Trancers*

3. *Bermuda Triangle* (1996), starring Jerry Hardin, TV's Deep Throat on *The X-Files*

4. *MacGyver: Lost Treasure of Atlantis* (1994), starring TV's Richard Dean Anderson and Brian Blessed

5. *The Man from Atlantis* (1977)

6. *Sharad of Atlantis* (1966), starring Lon Chaney, Jr.

Television Series

1. *Atlantis* (1985 miniseries)

2. *The Man from Atlantis* (1977–78), starring TV's Patrick Duffy and Victor Buono

(Source: Internet Movie Database, www.imdb.com)

Historical Atlantis

Where was the "real" Atlantis?

"EVERYTHING HAS TO BE SOMEWHERE," Thaddeus Thatch used to say when we would engage in the inevitable argument about some lost civilization or other. When the historical existence of Homer's Troy was proved in the mid-1870s, the revelation felt like a thunderbolt. Made Thatch giddy for three days. (Imagine if someone came to you today and said that the Emerald City had been discovered on the shores of Big Bear Lake.)

Over the centuries, many people, for various reasons, have theorized numerous geographic locations for Atlantis. Thatch knew that if anyone was ever going to find the city, the smartest place to start was Plato.[18]

The Greek philosopher wrote that the continent lay beyond the Pillars of Hercules (usually identified as the Straits of Gibraltar), where the Mediterranean Sea meets the Atlantic Ocean. Plato said, "Now in this island of Atlantis, there was a great and wonderful empire which had rule over the whole island and several others, and over parts of the continent, and, furthermore, the men of Atlantis had subjected the parts of Libya within the columns of Herakles[19] as far as Egypt, and of Europe as far as Tyrrhenia."

Now in fact, there were several "Pillars of Hercules" in antiquity—not only in Gibraltar, but also in Spain (Tartessus and Gadir), the Black Sea (the Bosporos), Arabia (the Babal-Mandab), and even as far as India (the Indus Delta). Wherever there were Greeks, there were "Pillars of Hercules." What does that mean? Interpretation—dear reader—construal, and explication! For the dreamer, it means the field is wide open, and a rationale can be created to locate Atlantis just about anywhere in the world![20]

Santorini, Thera, and the Minoan Civilization

Thera is the ancient name of the Cycladic island of Santorini (also called Thíra) in the southern Aegean Sea; it has an active volcano. In the middle of the second millennium B.C., an

---

[18] Other Greek thinkers, such as Aristotle and Pliny, disputed the existence of Atlantis, while Plutarch and Herodotus wrote of it as historical fact.

[19] Throughout writings on Atlantis you will see references to the Pillars of Herakles or Hercules. *Hercules* is the Latin name for the legendary Greek hero Herakles. The son of Zeus and Alcmene, Herakles was famed for his extraordinary strength and his many adventures.

[20] Here he goes again, cagey as can be....

explosive eruption with a force estimated to be three times greater than that of Krakatoa[21] buried Santorini's flourishing Bronze Age communities. Subsequent collapse of the magma chamber formed a sea-filled caldera, and left three small islands in place of the previous large one.

In 1899, seventy miles south of Santorini on the island of Crete, the British archaeologist Sir Arthur Evans unearthed a forgotten city of an important Bronze Age culture, which he called "Minoan" (after the legendary King Minos). Decades later, Greek archaeologist Spiradon Maranatos discovered evidence proving that the volcano of Santorini had erupted in 1,500 B.C. He theorized that Crete and modern Santorini had once been a single volcanic landmass before the explosive calamity.

In 1967, archaeologists uncovered an ancient city in the south of Santorini. The first building they excavated contained plumbing, toilets, and bathtubs. They also discovered rattan beds, ceramic pipes, frescoes, and other items that suggested a life of luxury. The archaeologists assumed the building to be a palace because of its affluence, but as soon as they excavated the next building, they found the same abundance and the same technological sophistication as in the first. They discovered that plumbing and sewage systems (including

---

[21] This volcanic eruption on August 27, 1883, along the Indonesian arc between Sumatra and Java, was the most violent explosion on Earth in modern times.

showers and hot and cold running water) honeycombed the *entire* lost city of Akrotiri. The more the archaeologists explored, the more objects they found (each room they discovered contained several hundred items). The more objects they found, the more the idea developed that this might have been the famous Atlantis.

Plato's descriptions fit Akrotiri well. In the *Critias*, he describes the water supply of Atlantis; the Atlanteans, he reports, had found a way of "bringing up two springs of water from beneath the earth, in gracious plenty flowing... fountains, one of cold and another of hot water.... [T]here were the king's baths and also the baths of private persons."

He wrote in the *Timaeus* of the wasted Atlantis, "a land carried 'round in a circle and disappeared in the depths below. By comparison to what then was, there are remaining in small islets only the bones of the wasted body, as they may be called, all the richer and softer parts of the soil having fallen away, and the mere skeleton of the country being left."

Many mythologists and archaeologists today cite Santorini and Crete as the most logical origin of the actual events that inspired the oral tradition that led to Plato's tale. Others believe the Minoans were really just trying to emulate what they'd heard about Atlantis in order to intimidate their neighbors into thinking they were more powerful than they actually were.

The Azores

It has also been proposed that the Azores are the peaks of the mountains of Atlantis, the only remains of the lost continent. A group of islands in the Atlantic Ocean, the Azores are located between 37 and 39 degrees north latitude, 740 miles west of southern Portugal. Nine islands (and the Formigas rocks), stretching from northwest to southeast over a distance of about 400 miles, make up the group. The small western islands, Corvo and Flores, are separated by about 150 miles of open sea from the central group, which consists of Faial, Pico, São Jorge, Graciosa, and Terceira. Open sea separates these from the southeastern islands of Sao Miguel and Santa Maria. The cluster of nine main islands is located amid a chain of underwater mountains that rise to heights in excess of 29,000 feet. They form part of the Mid-Atlantic Ridge, which defines the division between two tectonic plates, aligned approximately north–south beneath the ocean floor for some 10,000 miles. It is the tips of the very highest of these subterranean mountains that protrude from the ocean floor as the principal islands of the Azores. Even these tips possess conspicuous mountains that soar to a height in excess of 7,000 feet above sea level.[22]

Map of the Azores Islands from the Palazzo Pitti in Florence, Italy.

The Atlantic Island Theory

Well if there's a place that fairly cries out, "Plenty of room here for another continent," it's the mammoth expanse of the Atlantic Ocean, since it covers approximately twenty percent of the earth's surface. In fact, most people simply *assume* that

---

[22] Perhaps the most renowned proponent of the theory that the Azores are remnants of an Atlantean island continent was Ignatius Donnelly.

Cross-section of the Atlantic Ocean through the Azores (1923).

Atlantis lay between the Americas and Eurasia-Africa; and since, with its adjacent seas, the Atlantic Ocean occupies an area of about 41,100,000 square miles—well, as I said, there's plenty of room.

Many believe that Atlantis *must* have occupied the Atlantic Ocean, drawing this conclusion rather simply from the correlative name. However, we should recall, that ocean which the ancients called by the name *Atlantic*—or by others, such as *Outer Ocean, Mare Magnum, Mare Oceanum,* etc.— was not the same one we *now* know by that name.

The ancient "Atlantic Ocean" (or simply "Ocean") of the times of Plato, Herodotus, and Aristotle was the whole of an *earth-encircling* ocean. The ancients perceived the world, the lands they knew (Eurasia and Africa), as a roughly circular "plate" surrounded on all sides by an ocean (the "Atlantic"). Outside this circular ocean lay the true "continent," which in turn encircled the ocean all around. It is the old "flat earth" picture—you get the idea.

The Caribbean Sea

The Caribbean Sea is a partially enclosed body of water in the Western Hemisphere, a western extension of the Atlantic Ocean. It is bordered by South America (Venezuela, Colombia) on the south, Central America (Panama, Costa Rica, Nicaragua, Honduras, Guatemala, Belize, and Mexico) on the west, and the islands of the West Indies on the north and east.

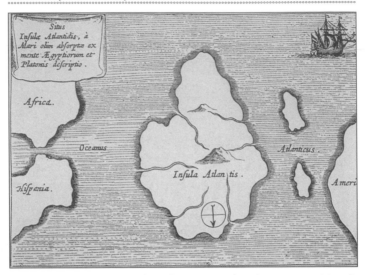

A seventeenth-century map by Athanasius Kircher showing a position for Atlantis relative to Europe, Africa, and America (albeit upside down).

The Yucatan Channel between Cuba and Yucatan connects the Caribbean Sea with the Gulf of Mexico, numerous passages between the islands join it to the Atlantic, and the Panama Canal furnishes access to the Pacific Ocean.

The West Indies, which form the nucleus of the Caribbean region, consist of two main groups: the Greater Antilles[23] (Cuba, Jamaica, Hispaniola, and Puerto Rico) to the north, and the Lesser Antilles (the Windward Islands and the Leeward Islands) to the east. The major channels separating the islands are Windward Passage, between Cuba and Hispaniola; the Mona Passage, between Hispaniola and Puerto Rico; and the Anegada Passage, between the British and U.S. Virgin Islands.

The total area of the Caribbean Sea is about 965,000 square miles. Several "ocean deeps" extend to depths greater than 23,000 feet. The greatest measured depth is the Bartlett Deep (23,744 ft) in the Cayman Trench between Cuba and Jamaica.

---

[23] The Antilles derive their name from a mythic island, Anthilia, for which Columbus was searching when he sailed the Caribbean Sea.

The Caribbean islands first piqued the curiosity of Atlantis seekers for a variety of reasons, including their adjacency to the Atlantic and the variety of shapes of the islands within the sea. Some evidence has been shown of primitive underwater walls and roads, now lying underwater.

Mariana Trench

The deepest point in all the oceans of the world, the Mariana Trench is located about 210 miles southwest of the island of Guam in the Pacific. At its deepest point, it measures 36,198 feet below sea level. The trench was formed by the phenomenon of subduction, whereby the ocean floor is constantly drawn down by the force of one tectonic plate being driven under another plate where the two collide along their edges.

But what if the cause of the subduction, as some have postulated, is something entirely different? What if some source of submarine energy is pulling at the floor of the ocean? Could residual power be continuing to be generated? Some theorists place the mythical land of Lemuria in this part of the Pacific. Could Lemuria be connected to Atlantis? Could this be a portal of some kind?

Great Britain

Plato's writings site Atlantis "west of the Pillars of Hercules," and it's interesting to note how far west of the Straits of Gibraltar some theorists of Atlantologists consider fair game—but Great Britain? This theory seems like a *real* stretch . . . although the Arthurian legend of the paradise island called Avalon off the British coast sounds awfully familiar. . . .

South America

After reading speculations that Atlantis might have existed in South America, former Royal Air Force cartographer J. M. Allen studied different translations of Plato's text, aerial photographs, and maps until he found a plain that seemed to mirror Plato's description. Allen writes in his book *Atlantis: The Andes Solution* (Windrush Press, 1998):

> *I began a systematic search of the Americas, looking for a place where the rectangular grid of canals would fit in. Only one location seemed appropriate and that was the Altiplano, or rather the portion of the Altiplano adjacent to Lake Poopó, for that was where the rectangular-shaped part of the Altiplano lay.*

Allen found many parallels between Bolivia's Lake Poopó area and Plato's descriptions:

- Lake Poopó's plain is surrounded by mountains and is high above the sea.
- The area nearby is rich in metals.
- The region's civilizations have a canal-building tradition.
- Using aerial photos, Allen found what appears to be a huge canal in the desert near the lake.
- Lake Poopó lies, as a footnote in one Plato translation mentions, "midway along the continent's greatest length."

Allan imagines that it was not the whole *island* of Atlantis that sank into the sea, but only its *city*. "What if it was not the island continent of Atlantis that sank into the sea, as Plato believed, but only the island *city* of Atlantis, built around the lava rings of an extinct or dormant volcano, which sank beneath an inland sea, or what is now Lake Poopó?"

Bermuda and the Bermuda Triangle

Bermuda is a British colony located in the Atlantic Ocean 600 miles east of Cape Hatteras, North Carolina. It consists of a twenty-two-mile-long chain of islands (approximately 150 of them) with an area of twenty-one square miles. The largest of the islands, Great Bermuda, is fourteen miles long and is connected by bridges to the other main island —

Somerset, Watford, Boaz, Ireland, St. George's, St. David's, and Coney.

Called the Sargasso Sea by Columbus, who was the first to note its strange, eerie properties, the Bermuda Triangle (also rather dramatically called the "Devil's Triangle") is an area of the Atlantic Ocean off southeast Florida, where the purported disappearance of ships and airplanes on a number of occasions has led to speculation about inexplicable turbulences and other atmospheric disturbances. Violent storms and downward air currents frequently occur there, but studies have not revealed any significant peculiarities about the area.

Some Atlantologists cite the boundaries of the triangle as the former location of Atlantis (the boundaries are formed by drawing an imaginary line from Melbourne, Florida, to Bermuda, to Puerto Rico, and back to Florida).

Prophet Edgar Cayce (more about him in "Spiritual Atlantis" later) believed that Atlanteans possessed remarkable technologies, including powerful "fire-crystals" which they harnessed for energy. He theorized that a disaster in which the fire-crystals went out of control was responsible for the cataclysm that destroyed Atlantis. Damaged fire-crystals, still active beneath the ocean waves, send out energy fields that interfere with passing ships and planes, which is how Cayce accounted for phenomena reported in the Bermuda Triangle.

The Bahamas and "The Bimini Road"

The Commonwealth of the Bahamas is composed of about 700 islands and more than 2,000 cays, islets, and rocks in the Atlantic Ocean about sixty miles off the southern Florida

coast. The Bahamas extend 760 miles southeastward to within fifty miles of Cuba. Their area is 5,382 square miles, spread over an area of more than 90,000 square miles of the Atlantic Ocean.

Edgar Cayce declared that the seat of Atlantis had been situated near the island of Bimini here, and prophesied that part of Atlantis would rise again to the surface in "1967 or 1968."

In a way, he was right, since in the summer of 1968, the occupants of a small plane flying off the coast of Florida saw strange shapes in the water below them. Hewn stones and fragments of manmade monuments of stone and marble that appeared to be laid out as a kind of crude "road" initially brought an enthusiastic response from Atlantologists. Their excitement was soon tempered by another theory: these disorderly fragments of varied objects and materials were most likely the discarded ballast stones of five centuries of ship traffic in the region.

East Indies

The countries of Burma, Thailand, Laos, Cambodia and Vietnam, as well as many islands (Indonesia, Malaysia, the Philippines, and Borneo) lie on a vast geologic plate known as the Sunda Shelf. This region has been proposed as the "real" location of Atlantis—but not in the configuration that exists today, where only the mountainous regions of the Shelf are exposed. This theory posits that, due to lower sea levels, the Sunda Shelf was an immense dry plain as big as North America during an ice age millennia ago.

Mount Shasta, California

Located in Northern California and soaring to a height of 14,162 feet, Mount Shasta is a dormant volcano in the Cascade mountain range (there are no recorded eruptions, but there are active hot springs). A secondary peak crests at 12,000 feet on the mountain's western slope, and above the timberline much of the mountain is covered with glaciers.

There have been reports that noted archaeologist Jerry Lee explored a vast interior chamber below the mountain, where he described finding a beautiful city with splendid marble homes, lovely parks, gardens, and trees. He is convinced that this is Atlantis. Or he could be as nutty as Aunt Aggie's Christmas Cake.

The Antarctic Theory

In their 1995 book, *When the Sky Fell: In Search of Atlantis*, Rand Flem-Ath and Rose Flem-Ath presented the theory that not only did an advanced civilization once exist on the continent now known as Antarctica but that it was probably destroyed in a global catastrophe that shifted the continent of Atlantis to its present position in about 9,600 B.C.

Where is that? The Flem-Aths contend that the combined evidence points convincingly to Antarctica, where the lost city of Atlantis lies under a blanket of impenetrable ice.

The authors used Charles Hapgood's theory of earth crust displacement[24] (which contends that at various stages in prehistory the earth's crust shifted dramatically, causing earthquakes, tidal waves, and devastating climatic changes) as the

---

[24] Hapgood was a history professor who published *Earth's Shifting Crust* (1958), in collaboration with James H. Campbell, a mathematician-engineer.

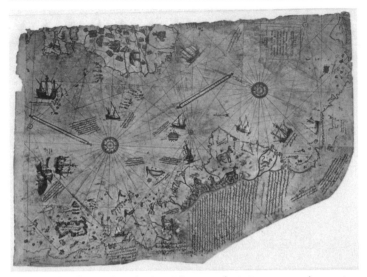

Some scholars have taken the Piri Re'is map of 1513 to suggest that ancient cartographers had both knowledge and skills not paralleled until modern times, since this map of Antartica without its glaciers is more accurate than explorers could have known at the time.

basis of their theory. The earth crust displacement model proposes that the earth's outer shell shifts, thus causing the polar ice sheets to move into warmer areas. The melting of these sheets causes a global flood, until a new polar ice sheet forms.

By studying ancient maps (Kircher's 1665 map of Atlantis, for instance, an amazingly accurate map of Antarctica *without* its ice), Plato's clues as to the location of Atlantis, and similarities between myths from around the world, the authors concluded that a civilization of intelligent seafarers *did* exist some 12,000 years ago but was destroyed by a geological disaster, leaving only a few survivors to pass on its legends to posterity.

As theories go, this one is plausible. Where is the last place on earth you would look for anything? Seems to me that makes Antarctica a logical place to look. Shackleton[25] seemed to think so, too. After being beaten to the South Pole

[25] Sir Ernest Henry Shackleton (1874–1922) was a British explorer. He wrote *The Heart of the Antarctic* (1909) and *South* (1919).

by Roald Amundsen,[26] why in heaven would he want to return? Shackleton's second voyage resulted in his ship, the *Endurance*, being crushed by the ice. The ensuing tale of survival and rescue is an astonishing one, and it has been rumored that those men encountered something there that helped them survive their ordeal. One theory is that a mysterious source revealed a way to harness energy from frozen ice crystals, which is just how the Atlanteans have been said to survive extreme cold.

Where is Atlantis, Anyway?

The Atlantic Ocean, the Azores, the Caribbean, Great Britain, South America, Bermuda, the Bahamas, Santorini, Crete, the East Indies, and the Antarctic: Atlantis has been sited just about everywhere where land meets sea—and many places where it doesn't.

The single *authentic* Atlantean location that everyone from scholars to armchair theorists can agree upon is in the *mind* of a revered Greek philosopher, gone from this earth for two millennia.

Plato gave life to the *idea* of Atlantis as an earthly paradise lost as punishment for worldly arrogance and carnal rapacity, a compelling concept that has permeated the thoughts of humankind ever since he wrote the *Timaeus* and the *Critias*.

No matter if Atlantis were discovered tomorrow, in many ways it could be nothing but a disappointment, a mundane shadow of our fantasies about it. Atlantis, like every paradise, has a greater home in our collective consciousness than it ever could in the physical world.

Does Atlantis exist? Certainly it does. And more than any earthbound physical artifact, the lost empire exists in the exhilarating and eternal realm of imagination.

---

[26] Roald Engelbregt Grauning Amundsen (1872–1928) was a Norwegian explorer who led the expedition that first reached the South Pole. Amundsen died while flying to the Arctic to rescue an Italian explorer, Umberto Nobile, from a dirigible crash.

The Atlantean People

Who lived in Atlantis?

I had a vision of a city on Atlantis. What a beautiful place! The streets were lined with fountains everywhere. Green trees, flowers, and park-like areas spaced the white marble buildings along boulevards. A temple crowned every hilltop, standing like sentinels guarding the populace, which they did. Each had a name and purpose and was visible from a large part of the city. They contained the governing bodies, the spiritual center, the healing center, the learning center, and the recreational center.

The entire city softly glowed from the bright sunlight reflecting on the white marble. This had a salubrious effect on the citizens, for they looked happy and contented as they made their way through the streets. The people wore colorful tunics, belted with a wide choice of materials. Sandals protected their feet, yet gave them access to the cool air. Most people were on foot, but occasionally the little airborne cars (hovercraft) would breeze by at a height of about eighteen feet. Sometimes those in the craft called greetings to those on the ground. The roofs of the public buildings acted as parking areas for these craft.

At the edge of the city just outside of the gates, acres of cultivated vegetable gardens and orchards stretched out over the land. Each morning the farmers brought their produce into the central warehouse. There seemed to be enough for all, as the climate was mild and conducive to abundant crops.

—from members of an Atlantis past-life regression group
in Seattle, May 1986

WHAT IS IT about Atlantis that so intrigues humankind? It's not just a big rock in the middle of the ocean that blew up who knows how many epochs ago. No, the compelling thing about Atlantis is its people, and how they lived, and what they built and created. Without its populace, Atlantis was, according to all descriptions, a very pretty island.

The First Age of Atlantis

The ancient island of Atlantis was composed of level plains and rolling hills, without extremes of mountain or valley. As hunter-gatherers, the early Atlanteans had a nomadic way of life.

In a warm climate that was conducive to lush vegetation, the Atlanteans eventually abandoned their nomadic ways and took up agriculture. At first they lived in caves or constructed high walls around their settlements to keep out wild animals. Later these walls kept out human invaders, but during this age, the Atlanteans did not engage in warfare. Survival and building a civilization was their primary activity,

and any combat was limited to defending themselves from predatory animals.

Early humans lived on two principal continents that are now under water: Lemuria[27] (thought to have existed in the Southern Pacific Ocean) and Atlantis. Lemurians and early Atlanteans learned from spiritual leaders. Most of the people of Atlantis followed whatever leader was present, and as long as spiritual leaders led, Atlantis progressed.

---

[27] Devotees of Lemuria claim that this is why paleontologists cannot find the earliest form of human—that those skeletal remains are at the bottom of the ocean. These same theorists claim that remains of other races and human giants are covered by ice in the northern and southern polar regions. They maintain that humankind will not find this physical evidence until a significant spiritual advancement takes place.

The Second Age of Atlantis

The first major climatic change was a movement of the polar regions that affected all of Earth's land masses and caused Lemuria to sink.[28] As Earth's tectonic plates shifted and volcanoes erupted, much of the fertile land and flourishing plant growth was submerged under water, replaced by sterile desert lands that arose, bringing about an ice age. As temperatures dropped and ice began forming on large areas of Earth's surface, droughts occurred.

The volcanic activity caused by this plate shift heavily polluted Earth's atmosphere and destroyed much of the protective ozone layer. The ultraviolet solar rays seared and destroyed. As less and less land became habitable, large populations were driven to colonize other, more hospitable areas of the Earth. The plunging temperatures forced human and animal populations toward the equator in search of a more accommodating climate.

Atlantis remained virtually unharmed by these global shifts, however, and its people often had to defend themselves from migrating hordes of exiled humans. The Atlantean defense against invading beasts became a refined defense

---

[28] Occasionally another ancient nation, Mu, is mentioned, but there is no historical, geological, or other physical evidence of it.

against invading men. Over time, the art of military resistance developed into offensive strategies and modes of conquest.

The civilization of Atlantis was not contrived to require leadership; consequently, there were few leaders.[29] Individual aptitude was assessed, and people were assigned to the areas where they were best suited. The original leaders and populace were spiritual and semi-ethereal, as Atlantis progressively evolved over eons into a sublime culture.

The Third Age of Atlantis

The Atlanteans' culture thrived and endured for many centuries, and they progressed in architecture, engineering, medicine, the arts, textiles, pottery, and handicrafts, and invented many scientific and mechanical marvels. By the time Earth was released from the grasp of the ice age, the culture of Atlantis was at its absolute zenith.

The Right Place at the Right Time

It has been said that during that first or second era in Atlantean history, tens of thousands of years ago, a giant comet passed close to the earth. A piece of this comet fell to earth in Atlantis. The otherwise normal race of people became extremely powerful when they discovered that the comet fragment possessed great properties.

The Atlanteans, it is theorized, found within this crystal and its fragments a manifold source of might that influenced every aspect of their entire lives and community, and protected them over millennia of peace and prosperity.

---

[29] Plato says that Atlantis was divided among ten priest-kings, who were in turn ruled by one high priest-king, who governed from the royal city.

Population

The *Critias* describes the manpower and division of the land in Atlantis. Other than the capital city, there were nine towns on the main island, each being responsible for an area of 10 by 10 stades (20,000 square yards), and each maintained a manpower detachment of 60,000 soldiers.

The royal city, as described by Plato, was the capital of an area of 3,000 by 2,000 stades (340 by 227 miles). If the other nine cities were about the same size, the whole of Atlantis would be about 30,000 by 20,000 stades (3,400 by 2,300 miles).

Applying the typical productivity of Asian agriculture (rice), an annual crop for a region of Plato's description would be approximately 10 to 20 million *tons* of rice and corresponding agricultural and pastoral products. This is enough rice and produce to feed a population of 15 to 30 million people—and still leave an ample surplus for export.[30]

The population of Atlantis can also be conjectured by Plato's discussion of its armed forces. Plato gives their number as 1,160,000 soldiers. If one half of the population was female, and half of the males were children, and one assumes that only a quarter of the adult male population was actually enlisted, it's fairly simple to tally a population of 20 million people (exactly in accord with the number estimated by the agricultural equation).

---

[30] Perhaps the cash export of such abundance afforded some of the legendary riches of Atlantis.

A population this size is *huge* according to the norms of the ancient world, especially if Plato is accurate and Atlantis flourished before the Neolithic Age. Just as Plato states, no nation of the age would have been so foolish as to challenge a behemoth like Atlantis.

How They Lived [31]

It is held that Atlantis was a Bronze Age nation, but one more advanced and cultured than other Bronze Age nations. Overall, it was a self-sustaining agricultural community,[32] capable of drawing medicinal liquids and gums from plants.

The Atlanteans knew hydraulic engineering and bridge building, and created many canals to irrigate their plains. They built many reservoirs and buildings, in addition to grand architecture. The capital was laid out in five concentric circles, with a great outer wall described as having a coating of brass, with a second, interior wall coated with tin, and a third wall sheathed in a now-unknown element then known

---

[31] Throughout the following section, Whitmore offers little or no attribution for the ideas he espouses, simply asserting these very explicit and convincing ideas on the strength of his narrative momentum. Cagey!

[32] Agriculture and animal domestication (as contrasted with hunting and gathering) are the two fundamental requisites for the development of city life and large, stable, civilized societies.

as oricalcum.

Atlantis was a literate and intelligent society, with a written language and laws. A court system assured that any citizen could bring a complaint or petition to be heard, and justice was meted out equitably by experienced judges, whose decisions were accepted without complaint by the populace. The law was a combination of common sense and spiritually motivated direction, with a goal of keeping the peoples' sights on caring for their neighbors and striving for the common good.

Toward that end, formalized education was fundamental, with schooling beginning at a young age with the central theme of enriching the mind while promoting a desire for more knowledge. Music, art, and dance played prominent roles in youth education, forming a framework for the integration of those skills with scientific and spiritual knowledge in the adolescent and older students.

Physical fitness was also taught from youth, and the elderly strove to keep fit. (Swimming was an important part of the physical fitness regimen, and a vital spiritual expression of the higher self in motion.)

Sports were also a vital component of Atlantean recreation. They included wrestling and other contests of strength, as well as various kinds of team sports (including a game similar to soccer), lawn bowling, footraces, and gymnastics. Sporting exhibitions, usually held in the arena with no admission fee, attracted many spectators. Many dance performances, music recitals, and poetry readings were staged at the arena.

Household pets were common—typically monkeys, birds, and small dogs upon whom their owners lavished much attention. Birds were taught to talk, and monkeys to perform tricks. People communicated with their animals through telepathy.

Most of all, it was a very easy and leisured society. For long ages, the Atlantean people appreciated their blessings of abundance and lived self-supported, and at peace with the rest of the world. They were untainted by their possessions and great wealth, and spent their lives engaged in activities of generosity and gentility. Their primary avocations were education, cultivating virtue, living in peace with each other and in harmony with nature.

Did the Atlanteans Abet Their Own Demise?

In time, the Atlanteans exercised their technological power to dominate other civilizations. They used the crystal to fuel a powerful armada of vehicles of war sculpted from exotic materials into the shape of sleek sea creatures—fish, sharks, and narwhals.

People began to neglect their work, and failed to train their children as they should. They bickered and quarreled among themselves, where before they had been peaceful. The populace began splitting into factions. Those practicing the rituals of virtue tried harder and harder to find solace within their temples. Those who did not were sucked into a vortex of fear and enslavement to their lower natures.

The destruction of Atlantis took place when it was contemplating a war of aggression with Athens and Egypt simultaneously. At the same time, an aggressive Athenian army was destroyed by natural calamity during the war.

The Atlanteans waged war with incredible strength, but their hubris caused a great accident to occur and the power of the crystals expunged them from the face of the earth.

In the *Timaeus*, Plato reports, "But afterwards there occurred violent earthquakes and floods; and in a single day and night of misfortune all your warlike men in a body sank into the earth, and the island of Atlantis in like manner disappeared in the depths of the sea."

Plato tells a more religious version of the Atlantis story in the *Critias*. There he describes the lost continent as the kingdom of Poseidon, the god of the sea. This Atlantis was a noble, sophisticated society that reigned in peace for centuries, until its people became complacent and greedy. Angered by their fall from grace, Zeus chose to punish them by destroying their beautiful paradise.

After the Calamity

Emissaries

Many theories of Atlantis hold that it was it a far-flung empire, part of a global shipping network with outposts throughout the known ancient world. An addendum to that theory is one which postulates that, in the face of the empire's impending demise, many Atlanteans chose to escape the destruction and act as emissaries of the Atlantean culture, spreading its centuries of accumulated knowledge and understanding all around the globe.[33]

Central and South American peoples claim to have been visited by a God (such as the Maya Votan, the Inca Viracocha, or the Aztec Quetzalcoatl) possessed of advanced technology, ideas, and teachings. This "deity" bore no physical resemblance to the natives (he had a straight nose, round eyes, and a beard and moustache), and is said to have arrived after "the darkening of the Sun." Could this visitor's "heavenly descent" actually have been the arrival of a refugee Atlantean seeking a new home after a calamity had destroyed his own?

The Maya (1500 B.C.–A.D. 1500)

With its peak period between the years of A.D. 250–900, the Mayan civilization numbered as many as 2,000,000 at one point and populated dozens of cities in what is now southern Mexico, Guatemala, and Belize. After the year 900, the Maya mysteriously depopulated much of their territory. Some say

---

[33] One theory says that the Basques, the original inhabitants of Spain and France, are the only survivors to escape Atlantis, and that is why they speak such a distinct tongue.

they were invaded and dominated by the Olmec of the north. The Maya encountered by the Spanish Conquistadors in the sixteenth century were a mere shadow of their ancestors.

The similarities in culture between Maya and Atlanteans aside, the parallel between the two civilizations' downfalls is fascinating. Both are said to have been flourishing beyond imagination. Both virtually vanished from the face of the Earth without explanation. What lesson do we have to learn from these peoples who flew so high on what appear now to have been borrowed wings?

Indus Valley Civilization (2500–1700 B.C.)

This large and advanced society grew up in an area roughly comprising northwest India. The inhabitants were a Dravidian people, whose descendents today live in southern India and Sri Lanka. They laid out their cities with streets in a grid pattern, and even introduced running water through clay pipes. They also had toilets and a sewer system not seen anywhere else in the world at the time. Scholars do not know how the society began, or where the people came from.

There are a lot of gaps in the history of this area. Where did its people really come from in the first place, and where did they go a thousand years later? The Indus Valley pictographic script remains undeciphered.[34] Could this have been one of the rumored Atlantean colonies?

---

[34] The Indus Valley script was finally deciphered in 1969.

Angkor Wat (A.D. 1100)

Glorious capital city of the Khmer Empire of Cambodia, Angkor Wat took thirty years to build and its design is an allegory on the Hindu worldview. The city includes such features as the world's longest bas-relief and a series of moats and lakes designed to represent the primordial ocean. How this amazing place came to be built in the middle of the jungle continues to perplex scholars. Of particular interest is the homage to the concept of a primordial ocean. In addition, this society came into its zenith as the Maya on the other side of the planet were in their final decline.

Jericho (8000 B.C.)

Located near the banks of the River Jordan, Jericho has the distinction of being the oldest known settlement on Earth, as well as being one of the lowest (800 feet below sea level). The establishment of the settlement marked a dramatic departure for a previously nomadic people. Jericho benefited from a system of irrigation and became a center of commerce and governance. The evolution of Jericho represents a very dramatic shift in how people lived, from a nomadic way of life to sophisticated trade, transportation, architecture, government, and irrigation. This cultural shift took place just after what many regard as the destruction of Atlantis. There have also been reports of fragments of a mysterious glasslike compound being found on the banks of the River Jordan not far from Jericho.

The Cloud People

In 1843, seventy years before the discovery of Machu Picchu made headlines, a mammoth ruin known as Kuelap (estimated to be constructed of twice as much building material as the Great Pyramid of Giza) was discovered in a remote and inaccessible location in northern Peru. It was built by the Chachapoya, or "Cloud People," whose remarkable civilization thrived until it was conquered by the Inca around A.D. 1475, after which it was decimated by the varied detrimental effects of Spanish colonial rule. Their descendants still live in this remote region, often in the shadow of the ancient ruins of their ancestors.

The ancient Chachapoya people have been said by some theorists to be tall, fair, and blue-eyed; others maintain that, although the Chachapoyans were indeed taller and rather different from the Incas, they were Amerindian, with no particular "Caucasoid" features. (The idea of these "tall, fair" natives may have originated in Spanish explorer Cieza de Leon's observation that the Chachapoyas were the "whitest" Indians in Peru.)

Explorer and author Gene Savoy is certain that ships were navigated along this region of the Amazon in Peru— ships easily capable of reaching Europe and Asia. This idea ties in with other common theories of an ancient time when a vast worldwide maritime network thrived, and with the idea that survivors of the Atlantean cataclysm spread far and wide throughout the world establishing new civilizations.

Those Who Stayed Behind

There is another school of thought about the fate of Atlantis, one that Thaddeus Thatch and his grandson, Milo Thatch, had found in their study of Atlantis and their pursuit of an obscure artifact known as "The Scrolls of Aziz" or "The Shepherd's Journal." The benevolent crystals are said to have saved Atlantis with a massive force field, but the holocaust drove Atlantis deep into the center of the earth and caused a great flood to sweep over all the earth.

The ancient leaders of Atlantis and in particular its king, Kashekem Nedakh, vowed to keep the power of the crystals a secret forever to prevent a recurrence of this traumatic event. The king ordered all accounts of the city's history destroyed and he hid the crystal deep beneath the city of Atlantis, where it was meant to stay forever. In time the Atlanteans became a peaceful tribal culture whose people lived along the water's edge in their lost underground city. Atlantis was a romantic ruin whose population lost track of their once great history.

Spiritual Atlantis

*Madame Blavatsky and the Theosophists,
Edgar Cayce, and others who sought
the answers to life's eternal questions
through the study of Atlantis*

*Indeed, the essence of the ancient Mystery Religions—from which
Christianity sprung—centered on the theme of Atlantis and its
demise in the cataclysm we call the Flood. The eschatology—that is,
the doctrine of final things such as Doom and the Resurrection of
the Dead—of Millenarian Religions such as Christianity,
Buddhism, and Hinduism all issue rather directly from the myths of
Atlantis and its terrible fate. So do traditions such as the Grail Cycle
and the myth of the Wandering Hero in search of Paradise. Indeed,
Atlantis is no other than the Primordial Paradise, which was the
source from where the gods and angels brought the Gospels and the
seeds of knowledge in the dawn of times.*

—Arysio Nuñes dos Santos

THE STORY OF ATLANTIS has been a spiritual one since Plato first set it down in the *Timaeus* and the *Critias*. Indeed, much of Plato's purpose in writing his dialogues was allegorical: he wanted to teach the danger of avarice, insolence, and cruelty and to illustrate the censure administered by heaven to those who worship false gods. Over the years, key elements of the story have occurred over and over again—man outcast from Paradise, punishing destruction of a colossal flood, a once-supreme society that has vanished overnight—making the Atlantis story a truly worldwide phenomenon. No matter the culture, if you relate the tale of Atlantis, you are bound to strike a familiar chord with your listener.

There are several key points in the story of Atlantis which recur in other stories and myths. The walled city of Atlantis is split into four by a canal system. The walled Garden of Eden had four rivers running through it. Many ancient South American cities are also based on this design, which is also said to have given rise to the garden style of the Persian kings, with a central pool of life, from which four rivers run in the form of a cross.

Plato's Atlantis had a vast network of canals used for irrigating the fertile plain from mountain waters, thus enabling two crops a year to be harvested. Similar engineering has been found in the ancient Far East and South America.

Madame Blavatsky and the Theosophists

Helena Petrovna Blavatsky, better known as Madame Blavatsky, was born on August 12, 1831, in the Ukraine. In 1849 she married N. V. Blavatsky, and shortly thereafter began more than twenty years of extensive travel, which brought her into contact with mystic traditions the world over. She would become one of the great proponents of the spiritual nature of the Atlantis legend, drawing the thread of its culturally common myths into a whole new spiritual definition of the renowned story.

Blavatsky arrived in New York in 1873. There was at that time a mania for Spiritualism, which is a philosophy whose adherents believe, as the basis of their religion, in the communication between this world and the spirit world by means of mediumship, and who endeavor to mold their character and conduct in accordance with the highest teachings derived from such communication.

Naturally, this philosophy, with its trappings of the mysterious and otherworldly, became something of a fad in the parlors and salons on Manhattan, where Spiritualism's more theatrical aspects were practiced for the amusement of the idle rich. Blavatsky established herself as a medium, presiding over seances and becoming a well-known celebrity or "character." Her psychic powers were widely acclaimed.[35]

In 1875, Blavatsky met Henry Steel Olcott, a former member of the committee that had investigated President Lincoln's assassination, and convinced him that they had been admitted to a secret order of cosmic masters (an order that included Christ, Buddha, Confucius, Solomon, and Plato).

Blavatsky's cosmic masters had arrived from another part of the universe to supervise the human race, and based themselves in Atlantis. After the destruction of the island continent, these masters had retreated to hidden valleys of the Himalayan mountains, where they watched the progress of man from afar. Blavatsky claimed to have spent several years in Tibet and India being initiated into occult mysteries by various "masters" (mahatmas or adepts)—especially the

---

[35] Her powers did not survive an investigation by the Society for Psychical Research, findings that are refuted by Theosophists to this day.

masters Morya and Koot Hoomi, who had "astral" bodies. These masters were known for their extraordinary psychic powers and were the sacred keepers of a mysterious "ancient wisdom." Blavatsky claimed to have been apprenticed to them for twenty years.

Now, they were instructing her to bring to humankind a new era of spiritual enlightenment, dedicated to universal brotherhood, the investigation of man's latent psychic powers, and bringing the philosophies of the Eastern world to the West. To this end, Blavatsky, Olcott and W. Q. Judge founded the Theosophical Society in New York City. In 1878 they relocated and carried on their work from India, where they worked to re-establish Oriental philosophical and religious ideas, largely through the pages of *The Theosophist*, a magazine that Blavatsky founded and edited.

Theosophy, or divine wisdom, refers either to the mysticism of philosophers who believe that they can understand the nature of God by direct apprehension, without revelation, or it refers to the esotericism of eclectic collectors of mystical and occult philosophies who claim to be handing down the great secrets of some ancient wisdom.[36]

In a footnote in her 1888 book, *The Secret Doctrine*, Madame Blavatsky states quite directly:

> *There was a time when the whole world, the totality of mankind, had one religion, and when they were of "one lip." "All the religions of the Earth were at first One and emanated from one centre," says Faber very truly.*

According to Blavatsky herself, "The chief aim of the . . . Theosophical Society [was] to reconcile all religions, sects and nations under a common system of ethics, based on eternal verities." She did not reject religions such as Christianity and

---

[36] "What was this 'Ancient Wisdom' which the theosophists promised to share?" *The Skeptic's Dictionary* asks. "It is truly an eclectic compilation of Hindu, Egyptian, Gnostic and other exotic scriptures and teachings, neo-Platonism, and stories like the Atlantis myth."

Hinduism, but claimed that all religions have an exoteric and an esoteric tradition. The exoteric traditions are unique and distinct for each religion. The esoteric doctrine is the same for all. She claimed to be passing on the wisdom of the *shared* esoteric doctrines.

Blavatsky left India under a cloud of suspicion in 1885, having been accused of faking materializations of teachings from her Masters. Blavatsky died in London in 1891 after many years of chronic illness.

Her harshest critics consider Madame Blavatsky to be one of most talented, clever, and interesting impostors in history. Her devoted followers consider her to be a saint and a genius. Since these traits are not mutually exclusive, it is quite possible she was both a fraud *and* a saintly genius.

Whatever her skills and whatever her motives, Blavatsky was canny in assessing the existence of the components of the Atlantis myths within collective consciousness. Whether her motives were truly spiritual or not is highly debatable, and to this day, Theosophists rabidly defend this idiosyncratic personality and her work.

Edgar Cayce

Edgar Cayce was born near Hopkinsville, Kentucky in 1877. He had little education and initially pursued a career in photography. After a "nervous collapse" at age nineteen, Cayce began to experience visions and receive messages prescribing ways to heal other people. Over a period of forty years, he performed "life readings" for and diagnosed more than 30,000 people. Cayce was known as "the sleeping prophet" because he would close his eyes and

Cataclisma *by Leonardo da Vinci (1452–1519)*

appear to go into a trance when he did his readings. His followers maintain that Cayce was able to tap into some sort of higher consciousness, such as God or the Akashic record, to get his psychic knowledge. Some of his more famous prophecies were that California will slide into the ocean and that New York City will be utterly destroyed in some sort of cataclysm.

Essential to his therapy was his belief that everyone has had previous existences, some going back thousands of years to Atlantis. Cayce is, in fact, one of the key modern proponents of the historical existence of Atlantis, including the idea that the Atlanteans possessed a great crystal, which Cayce referred to as the tuaoi stone. This he said was a huge cylindrical prism used to gather and focus energy, allowing the Atlanteans to do all kinds of fantastic things. The Atlanteans, overcome by worldly passions, misapplied the powers of their crystal and set off a chain of volcanic disturbances that led to the destruction of that ancient world. He predicted that in 1958 the U.S. government would discover a "death ray" that had been used on Atlantis.

Like the other Atlantean proxies Donnelly and Blavatsky before him, Cayce's celebrity lay as much in his personality as in his achievements. Cayce knew the value of an interesting public image and did little or nothing to stop public misconceptions about him. It is legend that an angel appeared to him when he was thirteen years old and asked him what his greatest desire was (Cayce allegedly told the angel that his greatest desire was to help people). He was purported to be able to absorb the contents of a book by putting it under his pillow while he slept. He was said to have passed spelling tests by using clairvoyance, since he was "illiterate and uneducated."[37]

Cayce died in 1945. Many of his reports were transcribed and preserved by the Association for Research and Enlightenment in Virginia Beach; these documents—and Cayce—were largely forgotten until publicized by a series of best-selling books published in the 1960s.

Ramtha

Ramtha is a 35,000-year-old Atlantean warrior-spirit that appeared in the kitchen of a Tacoma, Washington, woman in 1977. J. Z. Knight, who was born Judith Darlene Hampton in Roswell, New Mexico, says Ramtha first appeared to her about twenty five years ago as a dazzling display of purple light. The former cable-TV saleswoman has turned Ramtha into a multimillion-dollar spiritual empire that includes a publishing company, a bookstore, a clothing store, and a catalog business.

Knight claims that she is Ramtha's "channel," a conduit through which the ancient can enter the plane of this world. The pretty blonde woman goes into a trance and assumes a broad, masculine posture and body language and speaks a

---

[37] A zealous Cayce supporter at *The New York Times* is largely responsible for the illiteracy myth ("Illiterate Man Becomes a Doctor When Hypnotized," Sunday Magazine section, October 9, 1910).

kind of antediluvian English in a growling, throaty voice.

Knight say she once was "spiritually restless," but has been enlightened by Ramtha, an ancient being from Atlantis via Lemuria, since he first appeared to her while she was in business school.

Who is Ramtha? According to a Statement from Ramtha's School of Enlightenment (RSE):

> *Ramtha was from Lemuria. As a Lemurian he was one of a highly spiritual people, and a participant in a pilgrimage that traveled through what is now Mexico into the Atlantic basin (then Atlantis), which was the home of an advanced, technologically oriented civilization. The Lemurians were destitute people who were thought to be "soulless" by the Atlanteans (or "Atlatians" as Ramtha calls them), and subjected to the worst kinds of abuse. At the age of fourteen, he became a conqueror who freed his people from Atlantean tyranny. Ramtha became the greatest of all warriors, for his ignorance and hatred were overwhelming and he feared nothing. Many joined his crusade, and over the course of sixty-three years, he conquered two-thirds of the then known world. Traces of this march can be found in the remnants of ancient traditions: the great warrior was later to become "Rama" of the Hindu religion, the first god of the people of India. Late in his march, he was the recipient of a brutal assassination attempt. During his seven-year recovery process, he learned the mysteries of the unknown god and became enlightened. As a result of his enlightenment, he ascended in front of his people, promising his return.*
>
> *Ramtha has been commonly referred to in the media as a 35,000-year-old warrior from the lost continent of Atlantis. Some have referred to him as a Neanderthal or Cro-Magnon man due to the time period. This is not entirely the case. In Ramtha's cosmology, he very boldly*

states that mankind has been in existence a lot longer than the current conventional view held by science and that in fact mankind is millions of years old and that very advanced civilizations coexisted with lesser ones. Without entering into the debate about lost civilizations or anthropological findings, it is important to note that the conventional view is increasingly being challenged. Of late it has been discovered that mankind used tools as early as two million years B.C. The important element that is usually omitted from reports on Ramtha is that he is an individual who attained enlightenment, not unlike Gautama Buddha.

Ramtha's School of Enlightenment (RSE) is a school founded by and based on Ramtha and his teachings, which are nobly dedicated "to the study, development, and practical application of the divine, transcendental quality inherent in every person regardless of gender, creed, social status, or color of skin."

A lofty thought from Ramtha: "Do not try. Know. What you feel is what you know." [38]

Tribute to the Outlandish Crackpot

"Throughout history the true originator is always laughed at," Marian Paroo once said.[39] This detour into spiritual philosophies of Atlantis—apart from being informative and certainly entertaining—has not been without a greater purpose.

Anyone who intends to express a serious interest in the study of anything Atlantean had best be prepared for scorn and ridicule. You see, every true believer started out as an eccentric crackpot.

Whether its mastermind was Galileo, Columbus, Fulton,

---

[38] It may be Ramtha, but it sounds a lot like Yoda.

[39] Paroo was the town librarian in River City, Iowa at the time of Whitmore's original writing.

Edison, or Thatch, every great innovation has required a great innovative thinker who wasn't afraid of being called a nut.

There were many times when I doubted the sanity of my old friend Thaddeus Thatch as he went off on a wild ramble about the Shepherd's Journal or the rationale behind the Lemurian island theories.

His grandson, Milo, was subjected to humiliating indignities at the hands of his academic "colleagues." One of them even advised that if young Thatch continued his pursuits "chasing fairy tales" that he would "flush his career down the toilet just like his grandfather."

Innovation *demands* a certain screwball dedication that comes only from passion. It also requires the courage and strength to defend your passion and give your conviction life. That's how explorers are born.

Archaeological Atlantis

The search for physical evidence of the
Atlantean civilization, including the
Whitmore (and other) expeditions

"WHY DON'T YOU GO OUT and *find* the darn thing?" How many times my frustration at another of Thaddeus T. Thatch's "pursuits of the Grail"[40] ended with that phrase shouted across the table!

While my primary interest was the study of commerce and industry, Thatch was always fascinated with the fringes of archaeology. As often happens with the closest friends, our interests rubbed off on one another. He got me fascinated with history, antiquities, and relics; I got him fascinated with using my fortune to fund the expeditions to find them. In this fashion, we joined other explorers and archaeologists who have pursued the past.

---

[40] Whitmore is speaking figuratively. The rumor that he and Thatch had discovered the Holy Grail (the cup used at the last supper, in which Joseph of Arimathea gathered blood from Christ's wounds) has never been substantiated.

Archaeological expeditions to the Near East began in the early seventeenth century, when Pietro della Valle visited the ancient Persian capital of Persepolis, later studied by Jean Chardin (1643–1713) and Engelbert Kempfer (1651–1716).[41]

Using the Rosetta Stone, French Egyptologist Jean François Champollion was able to begin the decipherment of Egyptian hieroglyphics in 1822.

The first systematic excavations in the Near East took place in the nineteenth century. Paul Emile Botta began archaeological research at Khorsabad In 1843, and two years later A.H. Layard did the same at Nimrud.

The first scientific excavations were undertaken in 1880 at Giza under the supervision of Petrie.

From 1890 to 1900, an American expedition undertook excavations at Nippur; from 1899 to 1914, a German expedition to Babylon was led by Robert Koldewey; and significant findings were made Alalakh (Tell Atchana; 1912–1914) by Leonard Woolley.[42]

The brilliant German merchant-scientist Heinrich Schliemann, along with his friend and advisor, Wilhelm Dorpfeld, revealed the historicity of Homer's legendary Troy in 1872. In 1899, the English archaeologist Arthur Evans discovered the great palace at Knossos.[43]

In many ways, a sense of adventure looking for the long past seems odd in a world so seemingly consumed with a technological future, and the pursuit of something as seemingly fanciful as Atlantis seems even more lunatic. But our pursuit had an ancestor in the form of one of the great explorers of world history.

---

[41] Georg Friedrich Grotefend found the basis for the decoding of clay tablets containing Cuneiform writing at Persepolis by comparing them with the decipherment of inscriptions in three languages found at Behistun in Persia. The interpretation of cuneiform was completed in 1846 by H.C. Rawlinson.

[42] Woolley also explored Ur in Mesopotamia from 1922 to 1934.

[43] In 1952 an English architect and cryptographer, Michael Ventris, deciphered one of the two types of hieroglyphic script discovered by Evans at Knossos.

Columbus

Christopher Columbus was a multinational hero; an Italian-born navigator who sailed in the service of Spain, he is commonly described as having "discovered" America.

Columbus was not, however, the first European to cross the Atlantic. Documentary evidence supports claims that the Vikings reached the New World around A.D. 1000, and there is circumstantial evidence that both Portuguese and English fishing vessels made the crossing during the fourteenth century, probably landing in Newfoundland and Labrador. It appears that Columbus followed many Europeans who earlier had sailed westward across the Atlantic—though he sailed a different route. And although Columbus failed in his search for a westward route to Asia by sea, the discoveries he made were far more significant and valuable than the route he failed to find.

Columbus had heard of legendary Atlantic voyages and sailors' reports of "land to the *west* of Madeira and the Azores." Voraciously studying every book and map he could locate, Columbus accepted Marco Polo's (erroneous) location for Japan, 1,500 miles east of China; combined it with Ptolemy's (low) estimation of the circumference of the earth and (high) estimation of the size of the Eurasian landmass; and added the (faulty) suggestions of a Florentine cosmographer named Paolo dal Pozzo Toscanelli. Thus, Columbus came to believe that Japan was about 3,000 miles to the west of Portugal.

Not typically noted in the history books is another and somewhat more arcane motivation for Columbus' interest in

a western trade route. Some maintain that he was not looking for Asia at all, but a mythic land of great wealth that he
had heard about "from a one-eyed sailor in the Azores," a
magical lost paradise called Anthilia.

In 1485, after being refused support for an exploratory
voyage from King John II of Portugal, Columbus went to
Spain, where he spent almost seven years trying to gain
patronage from Queen Isabella I of Castile. Finally, in 1492,
terms for the expedition were set.

Columbus made four voyages—in 1492, 1493, 1498,
and 1502—sailing west from Spain throughout the West
Indies. It is said that he always believed that he had reached
Asia. (The greater achievement is that, having found the West
Indies after making such major errors in his navigational
computations and location, he was able not only to find his
way back to Europe, but to return to the Indies again and
again!)

Christopher Columbus died in Valladolid in 1506, never
having discovered the mythical Anthilia. However, the group
of islands that constitute all of the West Indies (except the
Bahamas) are still known by the name Columbus gave them:
the Antilles. Cuba, Jamaica, Hispaniola, and Puerto Rico
make up the Greater Antilles; while all the remaining islands
comprise the Lesser Antilles.

Adolf Hitler and the Raiders of the Lost Empire

A fascinating footnote to the exploration and archaeology of
Atlantis is the peculiar tale of a maniacal madman's fascination with the lost empire.

Adolf Hitler was the ruler of Germany from 1933 to 1945.
Guided by a racist ideology, he established a brutal totalitarian
regime under the ideological banner of National Socialism, or
Nazism. His drive for empire resulted in the appalling devas-
tation of World War II and the Holocaust, culminating in
Germany's defeat and the reordering of world power.

From the moment the Nazis seized power in 1933, they inaugurated archaeological and exploratory expeditions to search for historical sites, objects, and antiquities. Most historians and scholars considered these efforts ludicrous, lunatic-fringe research—for Hitler and his minions sought out relics like the Holy Grail and the Ark of the Covenant,[44] and evidence of the lost civilization of Atlantis.

Hitler had an obsession with such objects, artifacts, and places. Certainly he and his accomplices saw the golden publicity and propaganda value in their association with such potential finds, but Hitler himself was said to be fascinated with the secret occult knowledge and mystic power attached to such relics—including a belief that possession of such treasures would make his armies invincible.

In 1933 in Guatemala, a German expedition investigating a Mayan civilization reported finding skeletal remains of "nonhuman" beings that the locals claimed to be the lost peoples of Atlantis; the "find" was publicized throughout the German-speaking world in propaganda films.[45]

Nazism had several elements, primary among them a belief, with a theoretical and pseudoscientific basis in the works of Comte de Gobineau, Houston Stewart Chamberlain, and Alfred Rosenberg, in an Aryan German race superior to all others and destined to rule.

The devastation of World War I had ripped apart the German-speaking peoples of Europe. In reaction to this cultural splintering, the late 1920s saw the formation of a kind of celebratory Germanic popular culture. *Volksgruppen* celebrating the Nordic-German heritage in clubs, social organizations, and festivals became popular among the culturally disenfranchised German-speaking peoples throughout Europe.

---

[44] The Ark of the Covenant was originally a portable wooden chest containing the two stone tablets of the Ten Commandments. It was carried at the head of the column when the Jews fled from Egypt, and before their army in battle.

[45] The misshapen skulls were later discovered to be the result of an ancient head-binding ritual.

At the same time, various science-fiction writings began to appear on the subject of Atlantis. Novelist Edmund Kiß wrote a series of novels, including *The Glassy Sea, Spring in Atlantis*, and *Last Queen of Atlantis*, pseudoscientific fantasies with a sinister thesis: that a Nordic race had existed on Atlantis, a blond, blue-eyed, and superior civilization, the founders of European culture.

Kiß told the tale of an ice moon from deep space that collided with Earth, bringing with it the seed of Aryan man, naturally superior to the "ape-men" of the earth. These alien humanoids establish the first civilization on the planet, on the island continent of Atlantis.

The author's description of Atlantis closely resembled Plato's with one chilling exception: the spiritual temple at the center of the Atlantean metropolis had been transformed in the writings of Kiß into an office of war.

After another comet destroyed their island paradise, the Aryans of Atlantis migrated far to the north and were rejuvenated and reborn as the Germans, awaiting the day when a leader would come to resurrect the Aryan nation.

"Only time will tell where the limits of our power lie," Kiß wrote. "We must build a community that will demonstrate to all the visible signs of our Nordic blood. The whiteness of our skin, the blueness of our eyes, the freedom of our spirit uncorrupted by the base superstitions of religion."

This racist solemnization of a specious "superior origin" naturally tries to conceal its sinister side: the celebration of the Nordic ultimately leads to the legitimation of removing anything not Nordic.

Author Franz Wegener saw within the fragmentation and disaffection of the German peoples after World War I a definite cultural-psychological reason for the authors of these and other pseudoscientific books to look to the legends of Atlantis:

The yearning for the lost paradise like an island is explained by Jacques Lacan on the basis of child-development and psychoanalysis with "this premature separation that during birth removes the child from the womb and creates a lack that no motherly care can soften." In its further life, the child is anxious to reach again this secure, safe, prenatal condition. This longing for the uterus can later be sublimated by searching for a worldly lost paradise or also death.

The myth of the arch-mother makes use of the paradise-story of Atlantis as a carrier-structure. But this myth of the arch-mother itself carries as parasitarian, secondary, semiological system the abstractum death. Nevertheless, compared to other escapistic utopias of islands, the myth of Atlantis yet possesses the largest psychological authenticity because it also represents transparently the sublimation of death postulated by Lacan: The island sinks, people drown in the floods. The implicit longing for death, for 'decline,' is proved by . . . quotations in which the downfall is on the one hand welcomed laughingly, and is on the other hand considered — with the help of euphemistic attributes — as "gruesomely beautiful" and "wonderful."

Chilling. Now, let us shake off the sinister and return to the altruistic.

The Whitmore Expedition of 1914

The journal, the journal, that *doggone* Shepherd's Journal. Thaddeus Thatch was a man possessed, and it was that dang book that occupied most of his waking hours during his final years.

Now, the Shepherd's Journal itself is attributed to a shepherd named Aziz, and was first thought to be the writings of a madman, but later proved to be a detailed account of the shepherd's unbelievable encounter with a vast underground civilization that we believed to be none other than Atlantis.

I finally got so fed up with Thatch's raving about this journal that I funded an expedition to Iceland to find it. We brought it to Washington, D.C., for study, and here Thatch planned on translating the journal and publishing his findings in the *National Review of Archaeology and Science*, an important academic periodical. I was prepared to take the translated journal and mount an expedition to Atlantis, to honor Thatch and prove his genius to the world. Sadly, my good friend Thaddeus Thatch died on the return trip to Washington, leaving the cryptic journal in my possession, addressed to his grandson, **Milo James Thatch**. He said if anything were to happen to him, I should give it to Milo.

Thaddeus Thatch was a great man—the world has yet to realize how great. Those buffoons at the museum dragged him down and made a laughingstock of him. He died a broken man. If I could bring back just one shred of proof that his theories were valid, that would be  satisfactory for me. I knew that Milo Thatch was the key to such an expedition. (Thatch and a couple of million dollars' worth of hardware, anyway.)

Educated as a cartographer and linguist, young Thatch was nominally employed at the world's leading historical institution from 1903 to 1913. Aspiring to ascend to the ranks of his grandfather and stand among the great explorers of history, he was constantly frustrated by the trivial tasks his superiors would assign to him. Despite his enthusiastic and well-founded notions, his dreams of filling Thaddeus' shoes seemed distant indeed.

Thatch was also a bit meek, somewhat clumsy, and rather noticeably inept socially (probably due to his years of isolation in the museum's boiler room). Despite his outward awkwardness, however, Milo jumped at the chance to take part in an expedition to Atlantis, revealing the inner spirit that portends a greater man.

As far as the rest of the expedition crew, I got the best of the best. They are the same crew that brought the journal back.

Commander **Lyle Tiberius Rourke** was the pragmatic mercenary captain of the expedition. An old veteran of many campaigns for me, Rourke was tough and focused, although likeable, much as a charming but disreputable favorite uncle is likeable.

My assistant between the expeditions, **Helga Katrina Sinclair** served admirably as second in command to Captain Rourke. She was the "drill sergeant," facilitator, and "right

hand…man" for Rourke. Sinclair was quite a beauty too, and she learned to use her appearance combined with an aloof, verging on edgy, comportment much to her advantage—and to the advantage of any given task.

I had to bust **Vincenzo "Vinnie" Santorini** out of a Turkish prison. Vinny was the demolitions and explosives expert of the group; however, his personality was one of relaxed and unflappable calm. His previous occupation (florist) hadn't sparked him the way demolition did. Vinnie approached his job with the utmost professionalism. He appeared to be completely imperturbable, and to say that he was given to understatement is…an understatement. He also had a taste for a kind of nonchalant practical joke.

Gaetan Molière had a nose for dirt. Nicknamed "Mole," a French fellow, he was the expedition's geologist and tunneling expert. His admiration for the evolution of dirt, and singular respect for the delicate, untouched caverns was constantly put at odds with his own desire to burrow violently and gleefully through any obstacle he encountered. His thick spectacles and

round, squat body complemented his nickname. Mole was an expert on dirt the way some people are connoisseurs of fine wines.

Audrey Rocio Ramirez was just a pup, the youngest member of the expedition, but that fiery little gal had forgot-

ten more about engines than you and I will ever know—the grease-monkey mechanic of the team. She was cute as a button, but opinionated, and tended to be short-tempered with anyone of less mechanical expertise than herself—which was pretty much everyone. Best of all, she had a big heart and an admirable fearlessness in the face of danger.

Joshua Strongbear Sweet was the group's accomplished medic. Well versed in Western medicine and Arapaho healing, Sweet's fascination with—and endless discussion of—human biology caused nearly everyone in his presence to suffer bouts of nausea. Aside from this lapse of tact, Sweet was just as his name suggests, and a strong shoulder to lean on when things got tough.

While **Wilhelmina Bertha Packard** had worked variously as waitress, dance hall girl, and seamstress, her interests eventually took her into the newfangled field of electronic communication devices, where she was credited with several inventions and held several patents. Packard was the communications expert of the expedition. Something of a camera buff, she became the expedition's default photographer.

Jebidiah Allardyce "Cookie" Farnsworth was our old veteran cowpoke cook, whose years on the wagon train had made him the best road chef alive. He was irreverent and outspoken, and he had little patience with insults, especially when it concerned his cuisine. He was the ultimate culinary

cowboy, and luckily for me in my encounters with his work, I like lard.

I was awfully proud of the crew I had assembled, and I was just as proud of the armada I assembled—had a hand in designing the submarines, too—for this voyage of discovery.

The centerpiece of the fleet was the beautiful *Ulysses,* the 382-foot 18,750-ton armored deep-sea exploration submarine, the very first of her kind. Incorporating many advanced technologies not found in any other civilian or military vehicle of the time, she was developed by Whitmore Industries for the sole purpose of finding the lost city of Atlantis. Everything on the *Ulysses* was overbuilt and meant to survive the extremes of any situation it might encounter. She was made from a hybrid galvanized-iron alloy exclusively developed by Whitmore Industries.

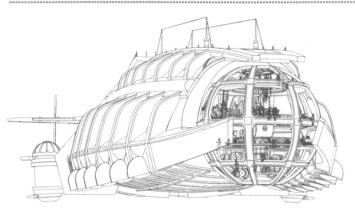

Her crew complement was 201, and her armament featured a dozen torpedo launchers with 180 degrees of movement, each armed with 120 DH-11 high-explosive proximity torpedoes.

Her primary propulsion was provided by four main SG-18 steam turbines with two shafts, providing 36,000 horsepower. A secondary propulsion unit consisted of ranks of high-efficiency rechargeable batteries with twelve hours of emergency power.

She also carried twenty-two independently launched attack subpods, compact miniature submarines intended for close-range attack and reconnaissance. They measured about twelve feet in length and weighed about 2,500 pounds in dry dock. These peppy two-person speedsters were powered by a single SG-4 electric turbine (single shaft) that provided 2,500 horsepower for a top speed of about twenty-two knots. The Subpods carried eight DH-4 mini-torpedoes and a pair of harpoon launchers.

The 120-foot, 62-ton Aqua-Evac (Aquatic Emergency Evacuation Craft) was used for transport of supplies, escape and for landing parties in areas that the *Ulysses* was too large to navigate to. It could carry several landing vehicles and their personnel (including supplies).

The Digger was Mole's pride and joy, a 56-foot, 112-ton, 5000 horsepower, land-based armored excavation vehicle fronted by a multi-bladed, high-speed excavation drill head composed of a diamond-infused hybrid steel alloy (patented by Whitmore Industries) with a maximum drilling speed of eight miles per hour. (Maximum road speed twenty miles per hour.)

Whitmore's Wing was a single-seat, ultralight aircraft intended for close-range reconnaissance or combat. It was very light and extremely maneuverable. Since it was launched from a catapult, it required less power than a plane that would need to take off from a runway. It was designed to glide to a hard landing on fixed skis upon completion of its mission.

The aircraft was mounted onto and launched from the Wing Launcher, essentially a modified transport truck with a height-adjustable steam pressure catapult in its bed.

The Tanker was a heavyweight truck with a 4000-gallon tank for transporting water. Hidden in the top third of the tank was the Gyro-Evac (Gyroscopic Evacuation airship) a 186-foot helium-filled airship with a powering turbine and a pair of counter-rotating propellers. The Gyro-Evac was a mobile inflatable field airship designed as a reconnaissance or emergency evacuation vehicle.

The Spanner was a heavy-duty special-purpose vehicle that could erect a temporary bridge up to one hundred feet long for traversing large drops and road gaps. The bridge was

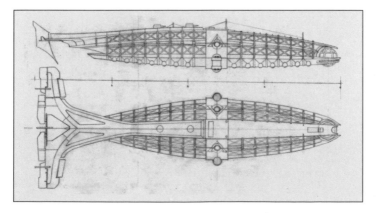

strong enough to support up to two heavy transport trucks crossing it at the same time.

With this spectacular complement of men and machinery, the expedition set off aboard the submarine *Ulysses*, with the Shepherd's Journal in the hands of Milo Thatch. As I watched with pride and anticipation, the great submarine boat submerged and began its descent to adventure and discovery. It was the last anyone would see of her.

Months later, what remained of my crack crew related a heartbreaking tale of mistranslations, misfortune, misadventure, missed opportunities. It appeared that the Shepherd's Journal was a deception. Although its basic information and Atlantean runes were authentic, it led the expedition in circles, and into terrifying hazards and frustrating dead ends.

For all its enthusiasm and wealth of assembled skill and technology, the Whitmore Expedition didn't find anything. In addition, it appeared that the expedition had cost the lives of hundreds of the *Ulysses*' crew and three of the expedition's important leaders.

What happened to Helga Sinclair? "Missing," the remaining crew said.

Rourke? "Missing, too."

What about Milo Thatch? "He went down with the sub."[46]

---

[46] We know now that Whitmore purposely obfuscated the facts of the mission for a number of reasons. Whitmore wrote, "A discovery of such magnitude, a power source of such enormity, and the damage the secrets of Atlantis could do to the world (let alone the danger it might cause those who were the custodians of those secrets)…well, the whole darn thing was just too dangerous to reveal to the world…especially the way the world was looking in those darkening days toward the end of 1914." The truth of the expedition has recently been made public, and the actual journal of Milo James Thatch has also surfaced.

Atlantean Artifacts

The physical objects of the archaeological
exploration, including
the legendary
Shepherd's
Journal

EVEN IN MY OWN FAILURE to prove its existence, I still believe that Atlantis is real. Part of that belief certainly has to do with my feelings for my friend, the brilliant and under-appreciated Thaddeus Thatch, as well as his equally brilliant and underappreciated grandson, Milo.

Part of that belief certainly has to do with the preponderance of philosophical and spiritual evidence and the impression that the very *idea* of this lost paradise has stamped itself on the collective consciousness of humankind over the centuries.

And part of that belief certainly has to do with the preponderance of remarkable evidence and artifacts that I have seen over many years.[47] While not the actual lost empire itself, there are too many interrelated relics for me to simply dismiss the connections between them.

---

[47] There have been reports of more that thirty ruins, including pyramids, domes, paved roads, rectangular buildings, columns, canals, and artifacts that have been found on the ocean floor from the Bahamas to the coasts of Europe and Africa.

Alexandria Lighthouse, 280 B.C.

One of the famed Seven Wonders of the World, the lighthouse soared 440 feet skyward from the island of Pharos in Alexandria harbor—taller than anything like it in its time. It stood until the fourteenth century, when it was destroyed by an earthquake. Magnificent and monumental, the lighthouse is another suspicious feat of engineering and architecture, in a time when *neither* had progressed far enough to build it. Why was it so tall? Certainly not just to warn ships…but for what other reason?

Stonehenge, 3000–1000 B.C.

Stonehenge is a prehistoric megalithic stone circle monument on the Salisbury plain in southern England. The monoliths that make up the circle come from Wales…240 *miles* distant. There are no natural building stones found within a dozen

miles of the circle. While theories abound, no researcher has yet been able to explain with certainty how Stonehenge came to be where it is, or why.

Little is mentioned about Atlantean spirituality or religion, but there are rumors of a "circle of masks" which collectively represent the Atlantean deity. The inhabitants of England at the time Stonehenge was constructed had limited means to create it. Could it have been built by a party of colonizing Atlanteans as a place of worship and inspiration—and a reminder of the great "mask circle" found in their homeland?

Pyramids

Pyramids can be found in several locations around the world, and have been built over many thousands of years. Perhaps the most famous pyramids are those found at Giza, Egypt; and at Teotihuacán and Chichén Itzá, Mexico.

Egyptian pyramids were massive tombs for dead rulers. Mexican pyramids served religious functions, and were often used in conjunction with grisly human sacrifices, which were a common component of the pre-Colombian religions.[48]

Some say pyramids housed sophisticated power-generat-

ing plants within their cores. Some say their configuration could reanimate the dead and preserve food and plants within their dimensions indefinitely. How did it come to pass that great clusters of pyramids have been constructed in such far-flung corners of the earth—seemingly unrelated to each other? Lost pages of the Shepherd's Journal (q.v.) are said to have pyramid shapes on them.[49]

Aztec Calendar

Discovered in 1790 beneath Mexico City, this round stone

---

[48] The Maya and Aztec reportedly told their conquerors that they came from Atlantis and Mu, and told them about ancient tablets (photographed in Peru) that show the two lost continents, Atlantis and Lemuria, as do several ancient maps.

[49] One Dr. Ray Brown reported exploring a pyramid on the sea floor off the Bahamas in 1970. Brown was accompanied by four divers who also found roads, domes, rectangular buildings, unidentified metallic instruments, and a statue holding a "mysterious" crystal containing miniature pyramids. The metal devices and crystal were reportedly taken to Florida for analysis at a university there, where it was discovered that the crystal amplified energy that passed through it.

calendar weighs about 25 tons and features a large sun symbol at its center. The calendar combined a ritual cycle of 260 days that ran alongside a solar cycle of 365 days. The calendar measured ritual and civil cycles, which repeated every 52 years. The calendar was used in the Aztec religion, keeping track of festival days and dictating when there were to be human sacrifices offered up to the gods.

Rosetta Stone (198 B.C.)

An Egyptian tablet discovered by the French in 1799, the Rosetta stone is famous for having permitted the decipherment of Egyptian heiroglyphics. The stone is inscribed with a royal decree commemorating the crowning of Ptolemy V Epiphanes, written in heiroglyphics, demotic Egyptian (the common tongue of the period), and Greek. It can be found in the British Museum.

This stone was carved by a truly gifted artisan. Though it has been exhaustively studied and is thought to be understood, there are those who are convinced that only a very small fraction of what this powerful stone can really do is known. It is rather a remarkable coincidence that the Shepherd's Journal and the Rosetta stone were pilfered by the British at the same time in Egypt. (Was someone attempting to use the Rosetta stone to unlock the secret of the journal?)

The Shepherd's Journal

This fascinating relic is said to be a firsthand account of Atlantis and its exact whereabouts.

One day a shepherd named Aziz was tending his flock near a mountainous region of what is now Syria when he slipped into a rift in the ground and disappeared. He returned a full two *years* later, babbling about an amazing place that he had found. He was branded a lunatic and thrown into an asylum, where he wrote a detailed account of his journey in a strange language that the people of his day thought was simply the mad nonsense and gibberish of a deluded crank. The scrolls came to be known in modern times as the Shepherd's Journal, and have been acknowledged by scholars to be an encrypted but detailed account of a journey to the ancient continent of Atlantis—actually written in the Atlantean language.

The Scrolls of Aziz

The Greeks were the first to study the journal, then known as the Scrolls of Aziz, and revealed them to be more fact than fiction. Plato knew of the existence of the scrolls from the Athenian statesman and lawgiver Solon, who believed the text of the journal (first thought to be a dead dialect from Mesopotamia) was actually written in Atlantean.

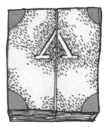

Scholars from the Roman Republic acquired the scrolls in Athens in the second century B.C. and brought them to Rome, where they were later plundered by the Franks (Gauls) in A.D. 290. Charlemagne, who briefly reunited the old Western and Eastern Roman Empires, had his advisors move the scrolls to Constantinople, with the intent of setting the best scholars in the Empire to try and decipher the journal.

A Turkish fortune hunter stole the scrolls from the libraries in Constantinople and headed west toward Iceland. On his journey he took ill on a tidal island called Lindisfarne off the coast of Northumberland, where he was cared for by local monks. When he died, he left them the scrolls, explaining their importance. In order to preserve the scrolls, the monks cut and bound them into journal format, adding meticulous and beautiful illuminations.

The Vikings and the New World

The Vikings plundered Lindisfarne in A.D. 793, taking the journal with them to Iceland, where they established an expedition to locate the mythical island of Atlantis. The Viking expedition was destroyed and the journal lost for a period of a hundred years. Thorfinn, the sole survivor of the Viking expedition, returned to Iceland, vowing to return the journal one day to its "rightful" home there. His followers were known as Keepers of the Journal.

The next documented appearance of the journal was in fifteenth-century Italy, but there is clear evidence that a bound manuscript matching the description of the journal existed in the New World around A.D. 1000. Some postulate that after the Viking expedition was destroyed, the journal was carried by the currents of the Atlantic Ocean toward Greenland. The Gulf Stream cast it far to the east, toward the northwestern coast of Africa. From there, the currents carried the Journal all the way across the Atlantic to the coast of the Yucatan Peninsula.

The more widely accepted explanation is that the journal was recovered by another Viking vessel and carried away, first to Iceland and later to the new-world Viking colony of Vinland in present-day Newfoundland. Here an Icelander named Snorri Karlsefni, said to be the first European child born in the New World, mounted an ill-fated trip westward looking for the city described in the journal. Along the way, Karlsefni traded with the indigenous people for furs; however relations with the natives turned hostile and two battles ensued. Karlsefni is likely to have bartered the journal away in exchange for safe passage home. But as a result of the animosity they encountered, the Norse abandoned their colony in the New World and sailed for home, leaving the journal behind.

For some time the whereabouts of the journal were unknown. It is next documented that the indigenous people (now known to be Maya) studied the images in the book to build some of their most memorable architecture, such as the reconstruction of Chichén Itzá.

Around 1200, when Chichén Itzá once again fell into ruin, the journal was taken far south to the present day Guyana region. Here a group of Maya, to escape the ritualistic sacrifices of humans by their leaders, had returned to a primitive culture without any form of writing so that the atrocities that transpired at Chichén Itzá would not be repeated. The journal went unused for two hundred years, and was more or less forgotten. All that was known (or handed down through the oral tradition) was that the journal was a book of great power—and possible evil!

Links to Europe

When the Portuguese explorer Amerigo Vespucci arrived in the New World in 1499, the tribe that he encountered, who were a Mayan people, gave him the journal. They considered it a gift of honor.

Vespucci could not decipher the language used in the journal, and spent many hours trying to understand its images, maps, and stories. However, Vespucci knew someone who might be able to decipher the journal. When Vespucci was growing up in Florence, in the 1460s and '70s, one of his friends was the brilliant Leonardo da Vinci. Upon returning from South "Amerigo" to Seville in the year 1500, he brought the journal to his lifelong friend, asking him to decipher it.

Da Vinci meticulously copied journal pages, and was perhaps the first modern man to fully translate the Atlantean language. He was particularly interested in the journal's scientific accounts of vehicular flight, and its assertion that the sun does not move—a theory that predates Copernicus and Galileo, and must have captivated da Vinci, since he wrote about it extensively in his notes. None of Leonardo's writings were published during his lifetime. He was left-handed, and after he saw the Journal, he had taken to writing from right to left so that his notes could only be read in a mirror. It was widely accepted that Leonardo was afraid of divulging his discoveries for fear that his writings would be controversial, if not heretical.

Against the wishes of da Vinci, the journal was confiscated. And, in a grand gesture that infuriated Vespucci, the journal was returned to Spain by the notorious adventurer Cesare Borgia, who sought to gain favor with Ferdinand V at the outset of the Spanish Inquisition. Ferdinand considered the journal heretical, but rather than destroying it, he hid it away in his castle. His grandson, Charles V, knew of the journal, but did not think much of it. Charles' son, who became King Phillip II of Spain (1556–1598), loved the mysterious journal, and during his reign, would proudly flaunt it at royal

functions. Phillip later used it as inspiration for the spires of his palace now known as the Escorial.

In the year 1589, Pope Sixtus V (1585–1590) rechristened the book the Shepherd's Journal, based on its ornate, almost religious illuminations. The Medici family acquired the journal from the Spanish royal family and returned it to Florence, where they added it to the growing collection at the Uffizi. It was English architect Christopher Wren who, in 1701, next unearthed the journal, still in the Uffizi in Florence. While on the grand tour, Wren stopped for a week in Florence in attempt to locate the journal. When he did, he solicited diplomatic help to secure a loan of the book to Cambridge University, where his brother was a professor in antiquities.

The journal stayed in Cambridge until it was summoned by George III, who begrudgingly gave it to Louis XVI of France and Marie Antoinette in a failed attempt to gain France's favor in England's dispute with the American colonies. In his diaries, American statesman, scientist, inventor, and writer Benjamin Franklin (1706–1790) mentions studying the journal during a visit to Versailles in 1788. All record of it was lost during the chaos of the French Revolution.

The Return to Iceland

Napoleon's troops recovered the long-lost journal in Egypt outside of Alexandria. It was stored there for a time with other artifacts, including the Rosetta stone, in preparation for their return to France. However, when Napoleon returned to Paris to deal with mounting political opposition, the British under Nelson and Abercrombie seized Napoleon's cache of archaeological artifacts and held them under the Treaty of 1800. The Egyptian artifacts were shipped with the British Fleet to Great Britain, where the journal was stored in the British Museum.

Scholars of the day thought the journal of no particular historical significance and it was given to the British Library. A visiting American senator of Irish ancestry named Ignatius Donnelly (q.v.), borrowed (and ultimately never returned) the manuscript. Donnelly was likely a "keeper" who used his diplomatic immunity to smuggle the journal to Ireland and eventually to Iceland around the mid-Nineteenth century. In 1880 Donnelly published a book called *Atlantis: The Antediluvian World* (q.v.) about the mysteries of Atlantis.

The journal remained in Iceland until the Whitmore-Thatch expedition retrieved it and brought it to Washington for study. Noted linguist Thaddeus Thatch planned to translate the journal and publish his findings in the *National Review of Archaeology and Science*. Sadly, Thatch died on the return trip to Washington.

Afterword

So, there you have it, dear readers, a succinct conspectus on one of the most compelling and fascinating ancient artifacts of humankind.

The skeptics among you are more skeptical than ever, no doubt. The true believers among you feel vindicated.

And the readers I most care about, the next generation of Thaddeus and Milo Thatches, have been inspired to dream, have been given permission to look at the remarkable and fascinating information contained within this volume, and may allow themselves to wonder.

About the Author

Preston B. Whitmore is the founder and sole owner of Preston Whitmore Industries, Ltd., an empire that encompasses logging operations in the states of Washington and Oregon; the Southern Rail Freight Line; Whitmore Mining and Petroleum in Texas, Alaska Territories, and South Africa; Whitmore Stockyards in Houston Texas; and PWI Shipbuilding in Norfolk Virginia. An avid collector of rare antiquities, Mr. Whitmore has spent sizeable fortunes on expeditions to retrieve precious relics, with the help of his longtime friend and advisor, Professor Thaddeus Thatch.

Adapted from
Walt Disney Pictures
Atlantis: The Lost Empire
Produced by Don Hahn
Directed by Gary Trousdale and Kirk Wise

Copyright © 2001 Disney Enterprises, Inc.

Text by Jeff Kurtti

ISBN: 0-7868-5326-3

Library of Congress Cataloging-in-Publication Data on file.

For information address:
Disney Editions, 114 Fifth Avenue, New York, New York 10011

Disney Editions Editorial Director: Wendy Lefkon
Disney Editions Senior Editor: Sara Baysinger
Disney Editions Assistant Editor: Jody Revenson
Disney Editions Copy Chief: Monica Mayper
Disney Editions Senior Copy Editor: Christopher Caines

Produced by:
Welcome Enterprises, Inc., 588 Broadway, New York, New York 10011.

Project Manager: Jacinta O'Halloran

Printed and bound in China by Toppan Printing Co., Inc.

First Edition

10 9 8 7 6 5 4 3 2 1

Visit www.disneyeditions.com

Art credits:
Page 9, 10, 18, 34, 36, 39, 40, Mary Evans Picture Library; page 14, Corbis/Gianni Dagli Orti; page 16, Foto Marburg/Art Resource, NY; pages 22, 24, 63, 65, 92, Corbis/Bettman; page 23, Corbis/Rykoff Collection; page 30, Marvel Comics Group; pages 38, 66, Scala/Art Resource, NY; page 58, Giraudon/Art Resource, NY; page 61, Art Resource, NY; page 73, SuperStock, Inc.; pages 85, 94, Academy of Natural Sciences of Philadelphia/Corbis.

Every attempt has been made to obtain permission to reproduce material protected by copyright. Where omissions may have occurred, the editor and publisher will be happy to acknowledge this in future printings.